How Can
I Believe
When
I Have
So Many
Doubts?

How Can
I Believe
When
I Have
So Many
Doubts?

Michael A. Babcock

HARVEST HOUSE PUBLISHERS

EUGENE, OREGON

Cover design by Koechel Peterson & Associates, Inc., Minneaplois, Minnesota

Cover photo © iStockphoto / Thinkstock

How Can I Believe When I Have So Many Doubts?
Copyright © 2011 by Michael A. Babcock
Published by Harvest House Publishers
Eugene, Oregon 97402
www.harvesthousepublishers.com

Library of Congress Cataloging-in-Publication Data

Babcock, Michael A.
How can I believe when I have so many doubts? / Michael A. Babcock.
    p. cm.
ISBN 978-0-7369-3073-4 (pbk.)
ISBN 978-0-7369-4037-5 (eBook)
1. Faith. 2. Christian life. I. Title.
BV4637.B23 2011
234'.23—dc22

                                                          2010031624

Printed in the United States of America

For my students—
that you may "grow in the grace and knowledge
of our Lord and Savior Jesus Christ" (2 Peter 3:18)

Contents

Part 2: How We Believe

Acknowledgments

Many friends have come alongside me over the years to encourage, challenge, and gently correct my shallow understanding of faith by their examples. I'll mention one friend, Steve Briggs, whose life has been a chalkboard for faith. Whether teaching pastors in a house church in Bhutan or lying in a hospital bed in Virginia, Steve has modeled a consistent, persevering faith. This book is richer because of his friendship.

My wife, Janel, and our children, Wesley and Mary, have endured "another book," and they have done so with patience and understanding. They deserve more than my thanks. Perhaps a vacation *without* draft copies of my next book stuffed into the luggage would be a good place to start.

Finally, I want to thank the publishing team at Harvest House for believing in a project I sometimes had many doubts about. It's been a blessing to work with them.

Introduction

IT'S OKAY TO DOUBT.

I wish someone had told me that when I was a young Christian. It might have spared me years of wandering in a wilderness where signposts had turned into question marks. I wish someone had told me that doubt can be a *good* thing—at least when it drives me back to God. It's good when doubt exposes the thin tissue of reason I'm standing on. I need to be reminded of my insufficiency. I need to remember how few answers I ever really hold in my hand.

I also wish someone had told me that *doubt is not the same as unbelief*—and that a faith that asks questions is stronger than a faith that never thinks. But that's just it. Nobody ever told me.

And that's why I've written this book. My goal, trust me, is not to sweep away your doubt with better arguments. My goal is not to build an unassailable fortress of logic—call it a "Faith Fortress"—that will leave all questions bouncing like rubber darts off the walls. My goal, in part, is to ask whether such a fortress could ever be built. To be sure, other books out there offer highly detailed blueprints, and even come with all the bricks and mortar you'll need if you want to tackle that kind of building project.

But consider this. If we could build that citadel, would we really want to flee there for refuge? There's always an underground canal that can be dammed up or diverted. There's always a sentry who's asleep on the night watch. There's always a bodyguard just looking for a bribe. Any fortress we make can be compromised, which is why the psalmist prays: "Lead me to the rock that is higher than I" (Psalm 61:2).

Doubt is necessary to faith, since our questioning is what drives us to God.

There's another problem with our Faith Fortress. Wouldn't we be giving up a part of who we are, a part of who God designed us to be, if we could ever build a fortress like this? And if we could shelter our faith behind some impregnable wall of logic, then what purpose would faith even serve? Instead of rendering doubt obsolete, we would manage only to make faith irrelevant—"and without faith it is impossible to please God" (Hebrews 11:6). The blunt and unavoidable theology of the matter is that doubt is necessary to faith, since our questioning is what drives us to God in the first place. "Anyone who comes to him," Hebrews tells us, "must believe that he exists and that he rewards those who earnestly seek him" (11:6).

You see, doubt is dealt with conclusively only by an encounter with the living God. That's why faith in a Person is the only answer to doubt. Not arguments. Not logic. Doubt, like suffering, is one of the tools God uses to whittle us down to size.

I remember an old Swiss missionary I knew as a child. He had spent years in Central Africa serving God and serving others. The one thing I remember most about him, apart from the warmth of his smile, was a little saying he often repeated—a play on words in the original French: *Ça dépend à ce qu'il pend* ("It depends on what it's hanging from."). The idiom means something like this: "Everything depends on the hook where it's hanging."

Our faith is like that. What hook does it hang from? The hook of logic and argumentation? Does my faith depend on Aristotle's law of noncontradiction or Anselm's ontological proof? Or does my faith hang on the character of God?

Maybe you're a skeptic. You've given up on faith altogether; you've resolved to depend upon yourself. If so, then I invite you to become reacquainted with the God who is faithful, who cannot lie, and who is worthy of our trust.

Or maybe you do believe, but questions continue to dog you. You're a closet doubter, and you sometimes wish you could seal off that little room, that closet inside your mind, where you manufacture questions that have no answers. Others seem to have no problem with their faith—and that's what bothers you most. God and the world clicks for them; but for you, the pieces always seem to be forced together. You imagine that you're the only one who thinks and feels this way, who asks these questions, who wonders why. Perhaps you even feel guilty for "just not having enough faith."

If that's you, then hang with me for a while. Start with one bit of good news: the pieces don't always snap into place. Doubt is an unavoidable part of who you are as a human being. You were made to doubt the easy answer, to wonder why things look the way they do, to speculate about alternative stories, and to entertain parallel universes in your mind. Your instinct to doubt is *natural,* even God-given.

Of course, it's hard sometimes to see doubt in such a positive and constructive way. All our experience with doubt tells us that it's a destructive force, one that unsettles and destabilizes our faith. Doubt seems to gnaw away at our spiritual vitality. How could anything good

When you doubt, you're in the best possible position to believe.

possibly come from it? We'll come to an answer for that. But until then, I'm asking you at the outset of this book to *trust* me—all irony aside—as we explore together the very human experience of doubting and believing.

In the following chapters I'll be pursuing three main goals. First, *I want to show how ordinary a thing doubt is*—how it emerges from our everyday circumstances. It isn't worthy of the stigma that Christians often attach to it or the mystique that skeptics sometimes dress it up in. It's just plain ordinary.

Second—and related to this—*our tendency to doubt, even as we yearn to believe, grows out of our dual nature as material and spiritual beings.* We doubt because we're made from the dust of the earth. We believe because God breathed into us the breath of life.

Third, *our questioning can actually promote the maturing of our faith.* But this happens only when our doubts turn us away from ourselves and drive us instead into the presence of an infinite God. Yes, doubt can turn to unbelief, just as temptation can turn to sin. But it doesn't have to. They're not the same thing.

And so to the question: *How can I believe when I have so many doubts?* I want you to see that when you doubt, you're in the best possible position to believe—the one God created for you, full of the richness of human experience with all its doubts and all its hopes. That's what we bring to God. That's all we ever bring to the One on whom all things depend.

Part 1

Why We Doubt

*"Then the Lord God formed the
man of dust from the ground."*
Genesis 2:7 esv

CHAPTER 1

Plain Ordinary

Key Idea: We'll never stop
asking questions because doubt
is a normal part of our lives.

"JUST LOOK AT THOSE ODD CREATURES!"

Tekla was pointing an arthritic finger at some sort of prickly blowfish with bulging eyes that was swimming, at that very moment, across her TV screen. It seemed she was always waiting up when I came home late from the university library. I wanted to slip in quietly—through the kitchen door and up to the single room I rented in the loft. I just wanted to go to bed. But she was lonely—a widow, an 80-year-old Swedish grandmother in an old working-class neighborhood in downtown Minneapolis.

She turned around in her La-Z-Boy just far enough to catch my eye as I entered through the dining room. "Do you really think God made all these strange creatures?" she said. And then her voice trailed off. "Sometimes I just wonder."

Sometimes I just wonder.

The ordinariness of her comment, the almost childlike candor, is what struck me most. Tekla came from that hardy Scandinavian stock that settled the Upper Midwest—hardworking, uncomplicated, Bible-believing Protestants. I'm pretty sure she would never have described her question as an expression of doubt. After all, she wasn't undergoing a crisis of faith. She hadn't reached the end of some philosophical argument driving her inexorably toward skepticism. Tekla was just watching a documentary on TV—nothing more—and she was puzzled by the wonders of creation. She had caught a glimpse of strange creatures lurking in the depths, and she asked the only question that made sense to her: *Why?*

Why, indeed, would God create such things? What purpose do they serve? I'm not sure there's a theologian anywhere who has a good answer to that.

Whether she realized it or not, Tekla was wrestling with the inscrutable mind of her Creator. Why would God make such monstrously beautiful creatures and then consign them to the depths of the ocean where few people could even appreciate his handiwork? Why should we have to rely on National Geographic to reveal the glory of God? Perhaps it's not a devastating question. But it's real and spontaneous. It's prompted by a simple observation of the world. Doubt is always like this. Doubt always springs from the soil of experience—or in Tekla's case, it swims up from the watery depths of our everyday lives.

That's how ordinary a thing doubt is. Somewhere along the way, we've lost the intuitive sense that doubt is part of the fabric of our lives. It's not to be shunned and it's not to be embraced with enthusiasm. *It just is.*

The mundane, unspectacular aspect of doubt is everywhere on display in the lives of the great faith heroes of the Bible. The earliest Christians too experienced doubt as the ordinary hand-in-glove reality of faith. How else do we explain the constant exhortations in the New Testament to maintain faith in the face of suffering? The modern Christian, however, has lost touch with the ancient understanding that we believe *despite our doubts*—that believing is actually the exercise of our will beyond the searchings of the mind and the frailties of the body.

Domesticating Doubt

"Do you think God made all these creatures?" Tekla asked again.

I smiled weakly and pretended that her question was merely rhetorical. Anyway, what could I say? I certainly had no answer. I was in my early twenties, a graduate student, and I thought I was smart enough to doubt everything I once believed as a child.

Just a few years earlier, as a 17-year-old Bible school student in Los Angeles, I had preached my first sermon at an alcohol rehab center. I don't remember my text or anything that I said. I just remember the bleary-eyed expressions on the faces of men who were not impressed by what I had to offer. Still, I preached with the confidence of one who *knew* what he believed.

But that was then. Now, a simple question about fish could undo me.

Mine had been an unspectacular path toward skepticism. Nothing dramatic happened. There was no crisis. Just the *drip, drip, drip* of unanswered questions. I had never learned as a young Christian how to handle my doubts. How to classify them, label them, figure out where to file them on the shelf. And with an unhealthy, unbalanced, and *unbiblical* view of doubt, I did what many young Christians end up doing: I drifted away from my faith and stopped thinking about it altogether. My own experience taught me that doubt, and our refusal to talk about it candidly, plays a significant role in our failure to thrive spiritually.

Big doubts are answered by a big God.

Doubt comes at us in many forms. We're familiar with the big doubts—the cosmic ones about the origin of life and the cultural ones about the truth claims of Christianity. We're familiar too with the personal doubts that hit us suddenly with that knock at the door, the phone call late at night, or the concerned look on the doctor's face. These questions usually top the list in any discussion of "the problem of doubt." Most books on Christian apologetics direct their fire against these targets, as though the doubting believer needs nothing more than good arguments to face down evolution, the Gnostic gospels, and a terminal illness.

But here's the problem. In many ways, it's easier to deal with the really big doubts than all the nagging little ones. Big doubts are answered by a big God. But what about my trivial doubts, those nagging questions that pop up like dandelions in the yard? How do I deal with these? Dandelions have a way of spreading. Before I know it, my nicely manicured lawn is overrun with them.

I envied how Tekla was able to turn off the TV and go to bed without giving a second thought to these odd little questions. Some of us can't do that. For us, the fish keep swimming in our brains. Questions are not so easily dismissed as idle curiosities. One set of questions leads us to another until we're staring blankly at the very foundations of our belief.

But looking back, I see that Tekla's question was a template for doubt. All our questions grow out of our interaction with the world. That's why we need to domesticate doubt—to wrestle it to the ground where it belongs. We need to deny its power over us and reject its mystique. The ordinary fact is that *we doubt because we're doubters.* It's the default position of men and women who are shaped out of the dust. We feel the earth in our very being; it pulls us, like gravity, toward earthly questions. In the pages that follow we'll be putting a basic formula to the test.

> *We doubt because we're formed from the dust.*
> *We believe because God breathed into us the breath of life.*

Domesticating doubt, accepting that it's just plain ordinary, is the first step to dealing with our questions about God, the world, and ourselves.

But what about the domestication of faith? I had to learn that faith too grows in the soil of everyday living. We do ourselves a great disservice when we cast doubt only against a great crisis, and when we cast faith only against the great tests we face. Yes, faith for Abraham was real in the extremities of his life, on the mountain when he lifted that dagger over the body of his son (Genesis 22). But faith was also real in the tents of his pilgrimage, each and every day as "he was looking forward to the city with foundations, whose architect and builder is God" (Hebrews 11:10).

Doubt is conquered by a personal encounter with the living God.

The church culture I grew up in believed that young Christians could deal decisively with their doubts by reading Josh McDowell or Francis Schaeffer. These men had done the heavy lifting for me. *They* had asked and answered all the hard questions. I could rest on the authority of *their* arguments. So the thinking went.

But as I grew in Christ—and continued to ask questions—I learned that doubt is not conquered by better arguments or better books on apologetics. Rather, *doubt is conquered by a personal encounter with the living God.*

God was relentless in his pursuit of me. Nothing remarkable had driven me away from faith, and my return to faith would be just as unremarkable. I would have to rethink what doubt is and rediscover the vibrancy and reckless-ness of faith. I would have to throw off the slogans of well-meaning believers and sound out the depths of a personal relationship with my Creator.

Only Believe?

The Christian who confesses to doubt is often answered with slogans: "Only believe!" and "Let go and let God!" I tried that approach too when I wasn't able to banish every doubt through arguments and evidence, through encyclopedic answers that had lots of footnotes. Perhaps I just had to flip the faith switch. Theologians call that view *fideism* (pronounced fee-DAY-ism), an awkward term built on the Latin word for faith, *fides*. Fideism, then, literally means "faith-ism," and it expresses a belief in the supremacy of faith over reason. It sounds good. After all, isn't faith superior to reason?

But there are many problems with this view. Fideism isn't heretical; it's just simplistic and misleading. It denies the full, biblical expression of who God created us to be. Fideism is alien to the kind of faith Paul described: "I know whom I have believed, and am convinced that he is able to guard what I have entrusted to him for that day" (2 Timothy 1:12). It's never "only believe" for Paul. It's "believe *first*—and then *know* and finally become *convinced.*" Paul always starts with someone who is worthy of trust. Reason is not rejected; rather, it is subordinated to our relationship with Christ.

> *Faith is always born out of desperation.*

The phrase "only believe" comes from Mark 5:35-36. A nobleman named Jairus approached Jesus with a desperate request. His little girl was dying. Would the Master come and heal her? As Jesus was being led to the nobleman's house, a woman pushed through the entourage and touched his clothing. Instantly, she was healed of a chronic hemorrhage. She too was in a desperate condition. She had spent years and a small fortune seeking a cure, but nothing had worked.

In both of these stories, faith is set against fear, not doubt. The woman is described as "trembling with fear," to which Jesus responded, "'Your faith has healed you'" (Mark 5:33-34). Before Jesus arrived at Jarius's house, servants came with the terrible news. The little girl had died. Jesus spoke before Jairus could even respond. "'Do not fear, only believe'" (Mark 5:36 ESV).

"Only believe" was the appropriate message for Jairus and the woman, because they had run out of options. They were afraid. Faith is always born out of desperation; it's not born out of an arbitrary decision, a casual choice to believe *this* instead of *that*. It's not produced by the victory of one logical argument over another. We must be brought to the end of our resources; we must realize that we were "dead in trespasses and sins" (Ephesians 2:1 NKJV). We must recognize that "at just the right time, when we were still powerless, Christ died for the ungodly" (Romans 5:6). This kind of desperation is necessary before we can get to the point where "only believe" makes any sense at all. One of the reasons the faith of so many fails is that it was never born out of desperation in the first place.

Let me give a well-known example. The story of Charles Blondin, a tightropewalker, is often cited as an example of what it means to believe. In 1859 Blondin stretched a tightrope a quarter of a mile across Niagara Falls and then crossed it several times, performing different feats. He went across on stilts, on a bicycle, and even asked if a volunteer was willing to be pushed across in a wheelbarrow. The story has been embellished many times, but the record seems to show that no spectator ever took the daredevil up on his offer.

Thousands had seen Blondin push the wheelbarrow across the tightrope while blindfolded, so they knew he was able to do it. In the usual pulpit version of this story, the failure of a single spectator to climb into the wheelbarrow was a failure of faith. But is this so? If Blondin had asked me to climb in, I would have said no too. Any reasonable person would say no. It would be a great act of foolhardiness to get into that wheelbarrow. What reason would I have for doing so?

But now change the circumstances a little. Consider for a moment that a raging forest fire has us trapped or that headhunting savages are rushing toward us. The only way of escape is across the tightrope. Would it then be so foolish to climb into the wheelbarrow? I've just seen Blondin cross the rope; I know my situation is desperate. All that remains is for me to commit myself to the single reasonable alternative before me, no matter how many doubts I might still have.

That kind of desperation brings us to God by faith. We don't come to him on a whim. We don't decide to cross the tightrope in a wheelbarrow because we have nothing better to do on a Sunday afternoon. We cross that rope because we've *come to the end of ourselves.* Only when we acknowledge the desperation of our condition can we really commit ourselves by faith to the wheelbarrow of God's grace. This is why "only believe" doesn't answer the skeptic's questions. The skeptic, like everyone else, must be utterly emptied of himself and flat out of options before he can reach out to God.

The more philosophical "leap of faith" isn't much of an improvement over

these popular slogans. A leap of faith con-
jures the picture of lemmings plunging
headlong to their deaths, for no good reason other than that the lemming in front
of them is doing it. That's the response
of a dogmatism that brings little thought
and reflection to its faith. And that's not
the kind of faith I want.

> *The moment of doubt is one of the great tipping points of the Christian life.*

A Tipping Point

So what's the answer for the doubting mind? Desperation. We've got
to reach a point—call it a tipping point—where we're ready and willing to
exercise a choice and step toward God. The moment of doubt is one of the
great tipping points of the Christian life. It's a moment of choice when we
turn either to faith or unbelief. Every question, big or small, thus becomes
an opportunity to exercise our faith in a fresh way.

We're programmed to ask questions, to seek answers, to wonder why. God
didn't make a mistake in creating us this way. It's real. It's human. It's who we
are. But what are we going to do with the capacity to doubt? Or better yet,
what are we going to let God do with it? That's where doubting and believing become a matter of our will.

Job reached that tipping point. And that's why he's one of the greatest
examples of faith in the Bible. You know the story—how a rich and righteous
man got caught up in a spiritual bidding war between God and Satan. "Job
only loves you because you've been good to him," Satan said. God then called
Satan's bluff by allowing him to afflict Job with sufferings and setbacks great
enough to shake his faith. Of course, God knew all along what Job's faith was
made of—and that's one of the encouraging subtexts of this story.

All of this is the frame of the story, given to us like a "behind the scenes"
documentary. Call it "The Making of Job"—*with never-before-seen footage
and candid interviews with God, Satan, and the Hosts of Heaven.* But we're
cheating in a sense, since we never get to peek behind the cosmic curtain
when we're going through this kind of suffering. We want a privileged view,
of course. We want a front-row seat to the counsels of God. Who doesn't? Job
gives us the next best thing.

God tells Satan to "consider my servant, Job." We too should consider his example. Job shows us how doubt, in all its ordinariness, can push us toward spiritual growth by deepening our humanity, our honesty, our humility, and our hope.

Consider My Servant

Job may well be the most anthropological book in the Bible. The book is an extended meditation on the mystery of being a human being in a world beyond our understanding. "'Naked I came from my mother's womb,'" Job said, "'and naked I will depart'" (Job 1:21). Job's friends came to comfort him, but instead they treated him like a sermon illustration. They canceled out the humanity of his condition with laws and interpretations. He was a living stigma to them, a breathing question mark about God. Sitting in sackcloth and ashes, Job troubled his friends greatly. They came to commiserate with him—Eliphaz, Bildad, Zophar, and Elihu—but they ended up explaining him away with theology. Not one of Job's counselors doubted God, but they all doubted Job. He was too human and too real.

We see no honesty in their faith either. Their sermonizing was inauthentic and shrill. How different it was when Abraham lodged a complaint against God for the impending judgment of Sodom and Gomorrah (Genesis 18:23). Or when Aaron was displeased with God over the deaths of his sons (Leviticus 10). Or when David took God to task for striking Uzzah dead (2 Samuel 6:8). They didn't understand God, but neither did they retreat into a sanctimonious defense of God's honor. None of these men settled for theological posturing. They struggled honestly with the Almighty—and they grew in faith.

The very fact of Job's suffering led his friends to deliver windy sermons on the godly life. They presumed to explain the mind of God, while denying the whole time that they were doing any such thing. There was no humility in their faith—only the arrogance of dogmatism.

There wasn't any hope either in what they said to Job. But Job's faith, by contrast, reached beyond his miserable circumstances to a glorious, if unseen, future. "'I know that my Redeemer lives,'" he said, "'and that in the end he will stand upon the earth'" (Job 19:25). Job's friends could summon nothing to match the scale of Job's hope. Theirs was a bleak legalism disguised as faith.

After 37 chapters, God grew weary of hearing theology thrown back at him. "'Who is this that darkens my counsel with words without knowledge?'"

Plain Ordinary

(38:2). Then God challenged Job to face his questions like a man (38:3). Job had brought his personal dilemma before the Almighty. A righteous man suddenly loses everything he has and is given no explanation. *Why?*

But God takes Job's question and rolls it up with every other question that has ever been asked. God responds to Job not by explaining to him why his children died or why the skin was falling off his bones. Instead, God starts speaking to him as though he's my old Swedish landlady. *Do you understand all the creatures I've made?* And God, like Tekla, has a point. If you Google "strange underwater creatures," you'll find all kinds of monsters you never knew existed. There's one called a viperfish—a really nasty thing that looks like it escaped from Steven Spielberg's art studio. Why on earth would God make such a creature?

Of course, Job isn't asking God about blowfish or viperfish. Job is asking, *Why am I suffering?* But God doesn't answer that question.

> *God must still defeat leviathan in the hearts of men and women today, and his main weapon for doing this is faith.*

Instead, he confronts Job with some strange, water-dwelling creatures such as *behemoth,* which is traditionally identified as a hippopotamus though all we can say for certain is that it is a powerful aquatic animal that eats grass.

> "Look at the behemoth,
>   which I made along with you
>   and which feeds on grass like an ox."
>   (Job 40:15)

I can imagine what Tekla would say: "Can you believe it? It looks like a cow, it chews on grass, but it lives in the water! What a strange creature!"

God also mentions *leviathan* (in Job 41:1), but we don't have any idea what this is. The term may be more symbolic than anything else, as the great sea creature that leviathan represents is found widely in the myths of ancient Semitic cultures. In the creation myths of Mesopotamia, El must defeat leviathan before order is established in creation. What a powerful image this is, especially since the spirit of leviathan is alive in our world—the spirit of chaos and disorder. This is the spirit that denies any higher Intelligence that rises above our own. God must still defeat leviathan in the hearts of men and women today, and his main weapon for doing this is faith.

Thomas Hobbes adopted the term *leviathan* as the title of his massive book, a dreary work of seventeenth-century philosophy that famously described human life as "solitary, poor, nasty, brutish, and short." Hobbes was one of the fathers of modern materialism—the belief that there is no reality beyond the physical, material world. He took this ancient mythic creature as his emblem, his representation of natural, humanistic, materialistic power. This leviathan too will be destroyed by God, along with every philosophy of man that challenges (as the Tower of Babel once did) God's sovereign reign. Every creature is subject to God's might and power—every strange creature exposed by National Geographic, but also our mythic creatures, our scientific fables, our secular nightmares, everything that swings its scaly tail against our faith each day.

The question of why God would create a blowfish might not keep us awake at night. But the suffering of a child, the inexplicable loss of a loved one, a sudden reversal of goodwill, cruelties that seem to go unpunished—these are the really tough questions. And God seems to take a pass on them all. He seems to answer the question of Job's life only with an endless interrogation of his own, as if to say, "You think you have questions? Man, you haven't even scratched the surface!"

But God is doing no such thing. Out of his majestic whirlwind, the Almighty gathers up every doubt, every objection, and drops them all into one little box that's been labeled by the finger of God. Open up the box called *Why?* and you'll find that God does not maintain a filing system for our doubts. There is no hierarchy of skepticism with God. Tekla's questions about blowfish are neither more trivial nor less personal than Job's questions about human suffering. And to that one generic question *Why?* God offers but a single answer: "'Everything under heaven belongs to me'" (Job 41:11).

The same God who was "reconciling the world to himself in Christ" (2 Corinthians 5:19) fashioned that little box out of the wood of the cross. And it was on that cross that the Son of Man and the Savior of mankind asked the deepest human question of all: "'My God, my God, why have you forsaken me?'" (Matthew 27:46). The stigma of my doubt, no less than the stigma of my sin, is closed away forever in the great Why of what Christ did.

Job has reached the tipping point—and he chooses faith. Consider the simple formula once again. It's important enough to repeat.

We doubt because we're material.
We believe because we're spiritual.

Job *doubted* because he sat in sackcloth and ashes. He *believed* because he knew that his Redeemer lives. Right there in that moment, Job looks up from the ashes of life, his body wracked by affliction, and he finds himself hurtling back toward his Maker. That's us—all of us—at the tipping point between doubt and faith.

My doubts too should always sling me back toward the infinite—and the infinitely *good*—heart of God. Only there, in the wide expanse of his Being, can my doubting heart find rest. Only there, in the intense fire of his presence, can my question marks be hammered and beaten and reforged into exclamation points of praise.

Summing-Up: There's nothing mysterious or alien about doubt. It's woven into the fabric of our lives. The example of Job shows us that we doubt because we're made of the dust of the earth. Whether our questions are big or small, they're motivated by the simple, ordinary desire to make sense of the world we live in.

For Further Reflection

1. What are some of the ordinary things in life that prompt questions in your mind?
2. Have you ever felt stigmatized by doubt? Do you feel free to talk about your doubts with other Christians?
3. Would you have volunteered to get in Blondin's wheelbarrow in 1859? Why or why not?
4. What times in your life would you describe as tipping points between faith and unbelief?

Chapter 2

The River of Doubt

Key Idea: Doubt is necessary and
even useful as we ask questions about
ourselves, others, and the world.

IT HAD BEEN A DIFFICULT YEAR, the kind that could shake the confidence of even the most supremely self-confident man. Teddy Roosevelt had spent 1912 on the campaign trail, pursuing a futile effort to take back the White House as a third-party candidate. Nothing was easy—nothing went right. After a campaign rally in Milwaukee, Wisconsin, a mentally imbalanced man named John Schrank stepped out of the crowd and shot Teddy at close range. The bullet was slowed down by a notebook in his front pocket, but it still lodged permanently in his chest.

That was the kind of year it had been.

So Teddy returned to what he called the "strenuous life" in the months following his defeat. He was incurably restless. He laid his speeches and his policy papers aside. Taking little more than his pride and John Schrank's bullet in his chest, he steamed toward the Southern Hemisphere. He was heading for South America, for adventure—and, in some respects, for personal redemption.

Roosevelt faced one of the greatest challenges of his life in Brazil—navigating a perilous, uncharted river known as the Rio da Dúvida, the "River of Doubt." He would later say that the adventure had taken ten years off his life. In fact, he died only five years after returning from the Amazon jungle.

When he wrote his account of the expedition, Roosevelt explained why the river had such an ominous name.

> On February 27, 1914, shortly after midday, we started down the River of Doubt into the unknown. We were quite uncertain whether after a week we should find ourselves in the Gy-Parana, or after six weeks in the Madeira, or after three months we knew not where. That was why the river was rightly christened the Dúvida.

"We were quite uncertain," Roosevelt wrote—and that has all the makings of a great adventure.

There was nothing uncertain about the origin of the river. That's where the journey began. Roosevelt was standing at the headwaters, deep in the jungle. And it was no mystery that the river had to empty somewhere into the Amazon—which it did, a thousand miles later, as an anonymous tributary.

So what was in doubt? Nobody knew how the beginning and the end fit together, because nobody knew what lay in between. All the uncharted rapids and unknown twists and turns were yet to be discovered. The middle was a mystery, a huge blank space on the map.

As long as we're held by time and space, we'll have questions we can't answer.

As Roosevelt placed his dugout into the water, he didn't know what would happen tomorrow or the next day. He didn't know, for example, that Julio would turn out to be a murderer. He had no idea that he, the former president of the United States, would stare down his own mortality and even contemplate taking an overdose of morphine to put himself out of his misery. "Anything could happen," Roosevelt wrote. "We were about to go into the unknown, and no one could say what it held."

It's Our Journey Too

Right from the outset, it's important for us to think clearly about doubt—about what it is and what it's not. We've already seen that doubt is normal. But is it necessary? Wouldn't we be better off if we could just sweep all our questions aside and live in a world of absolute certainty? Sure, there's adventure in not knowing where the rapids are going to take us; but wouldn't it be safer if the map were already filled in?

Here's the problem with that line of thinking. When you describe a world without doubt, you're no longer describing the world we live in. You're describing heaven—and we're not there yet. As long as we're bound by flesh and bones, we're stuck with doubt. As long as we're held by time and space, we'll have questions we can't answer.

This is our journey too. Like Roosevelt, we know what our starting point is. That much is certain, and we shouldn't ever forget it. Through the words of the prophets, God constantly reminded his people how they began as a nation. Everything started with faith and a promise.

> "Listen to me, you who pursue righteousness
>   and who seek the LORD:
> Look to the rock from which you were cut
>   and to the quarry from which you were hewn."
>   (Isaiah 51:1)

And then Isaiah goes on to describe that rock: "'Look to Abraham, your father'" (v. 2). Isaiah is not calling Israel to remember her ethnic identity; this is not an exhortation for Israel to make the family proud. Rather, Israel should remember how Abraham responded to the promises of God. Paul tells us that Abraham is "the father of all who believe" (Romans 4:11). That means we've been hewn from the rock of faith. Our journey began, like Abraham's, when God visited us in our tents and gave us a great promise.

Paul knew how his journey began one day on a dusty road to Damascus. Christ appeared to him in a vision and called him from unbelief to faith (Acts 9:1-19). It was a radical conversion for this man, Saul of Tarsus, who had persecuted the church and hated all that Jesus represented. Paul always came back to that starting place, because it always reminded him of the depths of God's grace.

Late in his life, Paul was able to say, "I was not disobedient to the vision from heaven" (Acts 26:19). He knew where he stood that first day on the Damascus Road. And he knew where he was going to end up. He had been given a great vision of the things God would bring about through his obedience. But Paul didn't know everything in between. God never gave him a detailed itinerary when he called him. God never does.

So, we know where we came from and where we're going, but we don't know the uncharted middle. We know by faith, however, that God is directing us from the beginning, through the middle, to a glorious end that he has prepared for us.

> And we know that in all things God works for the good of those who love him, who have been called according to his purpose. For those God foreknew he also predestined to be conformed to the likeness of his Son, that he might be the firstborn among many brothers. And those he predestined, he also called; those he called, he also justified; those he justified, he also glorified (Romans 8:28-30).

He knew us, predestined us, and called us; then he justified us and will someday glorify us. Because of this, we can have hope for the future. And few things can handle our doubts more effectively than an unshakable hope.

Doubt helps us define our limitations, protect our interests, and even make discoveries.

Hope is one of the hallmarks of the Christian life. We have the hope that Jesus is coming again. We have the hope of eternal life with God. Throughout the New Testament we are told to "watch and wait." We're pitching our tents in the direction of heaven. Those who would strip hope from our faith and reduce Christianity to a mere ethic, an elevated and noble code of conduct, have gutted Christianity of its very identity. We are a people of hope; we are saved by hope (Romans 8:24-25).

We know the beginning and the end. But we're still called to navigate down this river of doubt, flowing into uncharted territory and shedding years off our lives along the way. Doubt is unavoidable, but it can also help us as we journey down the river. In this chapter, we'll explore how doubt forces us to test the mettle of our lives, test the courage and reliability of others, and test the world around us as we map out its possibilities. Doubt thus helps us define our limitations, protect our interests, and even make discoveries. All this happens as we place our dugout into the river and launch out by faith into the unknown.

A Simple Definition

But first, it's time for a definition. We can all agree that doubt has to do with questions, uncertainties, and what-ifs. We know we're doubting when we ask why a lot. But let's try to simplify doubt even more.

Doubt is the consideration of alternatives.

That's it? Yes, I believe doubt always comes down to this, though we experience it in many different ways and at different levels of intensity. William James, the pioneering American psychologist, agreed when he said, "Faith means belief in something concerning which doubt is theoretically possible." I

> *The ability to doubt is a built-in feature of our original "factory design."*

believe X, even though Y and Z *could* be true. This way of thinking—of tracing out possibilities—is foundational to all human thought and experience in the world. We are constantly testing the boundaries of our certainty.

Every parent knows that children are hardwired for questions. Sometimes it's the annoying, repeated question ("Are we there yet?"). Sometimes the question is so profound—*out of the mouths of babes*—that it stops us in our tracks ("Where did God come from?"). A careful reading of Genesis 3 shows that the capacity to doubt, to consider alternatives, was already present in Adam and Eve before they fell into sin. If this is true, then the ability to doubt is a built-in feature of our original "factory design."

The serpent asked Adam and Eve to consider an alternative theory about God's nature. *Perhaps God is not so good after all. Perhaps God is really hiding something from you. He doesn't want the competition, so he's withholding this one fruit from you that will make you like gods* (Genesis 3:4-5).

The ability to ask questions didn't cause Adam and Eve to sin any more than the sex drive causes one to commit adultery. Rather, Adam and Eve sinned when they failed to turn those questions back around to what they already knew about God. They knew that God is good—and they should have said so. Satan's interrogation was a missed opportunity to bear witness to the truth and offer worship to their Creator.

We'll be looking at doubt from several angles in the chapters that lie ahead.

We'll also use a few metaphors along the way to help us picture what it's like to doubt—such as exploring an uncharted river, languishing in prison, and losing your footing. But I don't want to lose sight of this basic definition—that we doubt when we weigh alternative explanations.

We test alternatives in three areas of life, and these can be positive and productive experiences with doubt. *First,* I experience self-doubt when the inflated evaluation I hold of myself is challenged by the harsh realities around me. This kind of doubt should initiate a healthy process of self-analysis. Unless I doubt myself, I'll never be able to grow.

Second, when I suspect somebody of not being the person I thought he was, I begin to test alternative explanations for his motives and actions. If I had no capacity to doubt, then I couldn't spot deception and test character. Buying a used car or voting for a politician would be more hazardous activities than they already are without this capacity to doubt. I might end up e-mailing my bank account number to the widow of the president of Nigeria who needs my help in handling the estate.

Third, historical or scientific evidence may challenge me to consider alternatives to my fundamental beliefs. This can be the most troubling type of doubt as it drills down to the bedrock assumptions I make about the world. But I shouldn't fear these questions. After all, I want to know that the world isn't flat and doesn't rest on the back of a giant tortoise. Without the freedom to ask questions and weigh alternatives, scientific progress would be unthinkable.

Everywhere I turn, I am faced with alternatives. So let's look at each of these three types of questions more closely. As we do, we'll see that this definition of doubt places our questions squarely in the center of human experience. And that's exactly where they belong.

The Point of Nevertheless

Self-doubt is almost universally viewed as a bad thing. "Doubt whom you will," Christian Bovee said, "but never yourself." Bovee was a talented wordsmith—a nineteenth-century lawyer in New York who dabbled in literature and is remembered, to the extent that he is remembered at all, for his pithy one-liners. But the danger with a good quote is that it manages to sound good even when it says nothing. Bovee would have done well to disregard his own advice. Only a fool never doubts himself.

The capacity to doubt ourselves is both normal and necessary. We start life with a wildly inflated self-concept. Then we get whittled down to size through the hard friction of living. At some point you find yourself crouching on the eaves of a garage roof, as I did at age five, flight-ready with cardboard wings strapped to my arms. I was ready to fly, like Icarus—or rather, to fall to the earth. The several feet weren't enough to injure me, but the experience was enough to initiate self-doubt.

And this is good. That's what I needed. The distance between our perch and the ground grows wider the older we get, and so we wouldn't want to go through life thinking we can fly.

> *Self-doubt is one of the refining tools God uses to prepare his servants for ministry.*

This capacity to doubt myself, painful and humiliating though it is, has been built into me. Throughout Scripture, we see that self-doubt is one of the refining tools God uses to prepare his servants for ministry. As a spokesman for the world's wisdom, Bovee tells us not to doubt ourselves. The Bible tells us that we *must* doubt ourselves completely, or we're no use to God. You see, we don't fully understand the motives of our own hearts. We don't easily recognize the limitations of our knowledge.

The ancient Greek philosophers knew this. That's why Socrates is much admired for his confession of ignorance. "The one thing I know," he said, "is that I don't know anything." The Greeks believed that true knowledge begins with an understanding of the self. Philosophy was thus developed as a rigorous method of self-analysis. You were *meant* to doubt yourself as the first step to wisdom; you were supposed to acknowledge your own ignorance. But that doesn't necessarily make you humble. No doubt there was a fair amount of pride in what Socrates said. I'm guessing he really meant something like, "I'm ignorant, but not so much as you. At least I *know* I'm ignorant." Most of the Greek philosophers were pretty smug that way.

We're called to a very different kind of humility; it's a humility produced by a genuine self-doubt, not a public pose. David's knowledge of his own shortcomings grew in direct proportion to his knowledge of God.

> "Show me, O LORD, my life's end
>> and the number of my days;
>> let me know how fleeting is my life.
> You have made my days a mere handbreadth;
>> the span of my years is as nothing before you.
> Each man's life is but a breath."
>
> (Psalm 39:4-5)

David knew that he didn't fully understand his own heart. That's why he didn't rely on his own methods of self-analysis.

> Search me, O God, and know my heart;
>> test me and know my anxious thoughts.
> See if there is any offensive way in me,
>> and lead me in the way everlasting.
>
> (Psalm 139:23-24)

Greek philosophy—and its modern outgrowth, the scientific method— became the secular instrument for studying and evaluating the self. But this is essentially the fox guarding the henhouse. The self is protecting its own interests. Socrates professes humility, but he's really wearing a mask.

Martyn Lloyd-Jones wrote that "the secret of a successful spiritual life" lies in two things: "I must have complete, absolute confidence in God, and no confidence in myself." Psalm 46:10 tells us, "'Be still, and know that I am God.'" This isn't a call to silence; it's a call to weakness. The root of the Hebrew verb means to let our hands drop down, as though disheartened. We must come to the end of ourselves before we can "know that he is God." That's why Paul said, "I will boast all the more gladly about my weaknesses, so that Christ's power may rest on me" (2 Corinthians 12:9).

Jesus had to bring his disciples to the point of inadequacy, to the point where they doubted themselves, before they could learn to trust in him. Peter was an especially tough case. Imagine the scene when Jesus walked up to the shore where Peter was fishing. The Galilean water gently lapped up over Jesus' sandals as he watched the tired fishermen pulling in their empty nets. If Peter knew anything in the world, it was how to fish. But he had toiled all night and had nothing to show for it. So it must have been hard to restrain himself when Jesus told them to let down the nets one more time.

Peter probably felt as I do when I call the toll-free customer service line to get technical help when the wireless router isn't working properly. The first question I'm asked always is a bit insulting to me, but I know it's necessary. I know it's part of the script. "Have you checked to make sure the router is plugged in?" Imagine how foolish it must have sounded to Peter when Jesus said, "Put down your nets on the other side." Of course, Peter had been letting down the net on both sides. *Yes, he had plugged in the router!*

> *God takes self-confident people and grinds them down to the point of doubt.*

I wonder if Peter was just humoring Jesus. "'Master,'" he said, "'we have toiled all night and caught nothing; nevertheless at Your word I will let down the net'" (Luke 5:5 NKJV). Yes, Peter obeys, but only after he's made his point, established his credentials, and registered his doubt. But in the end he says, "Nevertheless, I will."

This is no blind faith on Peter's part, and that's why it's powerful. Jesus doesn't rebuke him, because Peter is just learning to doubt his own ability. He'll have many more opportunities to come to the end of himself. But for now, he's taking the first step toward trusting Christ implicitly.

God's work in our lives always begins on the foundation of a nevertheless. Peter needed to doubt himself. He had to face the alternative that he could be wrong about the very things he grasped tightly in his hand. *I hold this net. It defines me. I know fishing inside and out. I'm not a carpenter like Jesus; I'm a fisherman, and I know this lake. Certainly, that knowledge and experience must count for something! Nevertheless, nevertheless. . .*

What happens next? Peter pulls up a record catch—enough to fill two boats to the point of sinking—and he falls down before Christ. "'Depart from me,'" he says, "'for I am a sinful man, O Lord!'" (Luke 5:8 NKJV). In our self-confidence, we think we somehow belong in God's presence. We might even think that God needs our expertise, our experience, our knack for finding the best fishing holes. But Peter got it right. He began to doubt himself.

All through Scripture the pattern repeats itself. God takes self-confident people—Joseph, Moses, David, Paul—and he grinds them down to the point of doubt. Only then can the work of faith really begin. Every doubt I have should bring me back to the point of "nevertheless," back to the place where it all began, the time when I first trusted God in spite of everything that my mind or heart was telling me.

But there's another way we consider alternatives. We doubt other people too. And just like self-doubt, this too is normal and necessary.

What Charlie Didn't Know

I've always loved Alfred Hitchcock's films—those dark, quirky explorations of the human soul and the American suburb. *Shadow of a Doubt,* Hitchcock's personal favorite, is an exposé of the darkness lurking beneath the ordinariness of a small American town, Santa Rosa, California. It's vintage Hitchcock. All the twists and turns, all the sardonic humor and perverse irony are there. And, of course, Hitchcock is there too as he makes his trademark cameo appearance on the train to Santa Rosa. He's the fat man playing cards.

Shadow is Hitchcock's most American film. The screenplay was written by Thornton Wilder, the Pulitzer-prize winning author of *Our Town.* The homes in Santa Rosa are identical. The lawns are nicely manicured. The streets are lined with shade trees. Everything is middle-class perfect—except that a murderer has blended into the innocuous landscape, and nobody has noticed.

The story is told from the perspective of a teenage girl, nicknamed Charlie, who idolizes her namesake. Uncle Charlie is everything the small-town girl wants to be—sophisticated, suave, and well-traveled. But we've seen something at the beginning of the film that the girl didn't know. We saw Uncle Charlie murder a woman for her money. When the uncle arrives in Santa Rosa for a visit, he's actually on the run from the law.

Uncle Charlie's moodiness and eccentricities are casually explained away by his family members. Nobody imagines that he could be a ruthless serial killer. But eventually his past catches up with him. A detective arrives in town and begins to ask young Charlie about her uncle. She is confronted with doubts. Could the uncle she looks up to really be the Merry Widow Murderer? She decides to find out—to get closer to Uncle Charlie and see what she can determine for herself. The evidence mounts, and Charlie can no longer escape the truth. In a dizzying finale that only Hitchcock could orchestrate, Uncle Charlie tries to kill his suspicious niece before he himself falls to his death in front of an oncoming train.

Hitchcock's films are parables of certainty and doubt—chilling reminders that we often don't have a clue what's going on in the mind or heart of the person standing next to us. Teddy Roosevelt's expeditionary team turned out to include a murderer too. One of the porters, Julio, shot a man in an argument and slowed down the team as they searched unsuccessfully for him in the jungle. Of course, Julio never would have been hired if his true character had been known.

We've harnessed the power of science in an effort to limit doubts about character. Lie-detector tests gauge our physiological reactions as we answer questions. Our heart rate and the moisture on our skin can be telling indications of truth or falsehood. Personality profile tests put us through a battery of questions in order to determine our character—our propensity, say, to embezzle from the company or harass fellow employees. Profilers use behavior templates, developed from intricate statistical analysis, to track criminals. Some think that genetic data may be used to take criminal profiling to an entirely new level. As sophisticated as these techniques are, they're not foolproof guards against deception.

This capacity to be suspicious of people is important too for the purity of the church. Jesus warned about wolves that will enter into the flock to deceive and devour. We should watch carefully, he said, and judge the quality of their fruit (Matthew 7:15-20). We should not be gullible, but cautious and prudent. "'Therefore be as shrewd as snakes,'" Jesus said, "'and as innocent as doves'" (Matthew 10:16).

Our doubts push us to map and remap the world we live in.

These examples remind us that doubting is a normal function of the human mind. We normally think of doubt in exclusively negative terms, and fail to see how asking questions, challenging appearances, and probing beneath the surface can be highly productive. Once again, we need to domesticate doubt; we need to recognize that it's both normal and necessary to ask questions about ourselves and about others.

The Road to Doubt

Often, we're forced to question our basic assumptions about the world. We have a theory about which way the river flows; but then we find, like Roosevelt, that the reality is quite different from what we first expected. Our doubts push us to map and remap the world we live in. This can be good; it can lead to tangible progress and scientific advance.

It can also be traumatic.

Sometimes our doubts about the world lead to a complete reversal in our thinking and can even precipitate a change in worldview. This happened on a big scale when Nicolaus Copernicus, the sixteenth-century Polish astronomer, challenged the long-held belief that the earth is the central point in the universe.

Sometimes, though, our beliefs are shaken to the core only to be reaffirmed and come out stronger. We see an example of this kind of doubt in a story that only Luke relates.

Two disciples found themselves journeying not on the river of doubt but on the road to doubt, the Road to Emmaus. Jesus joined them for a walk, which is itself a beautiful picture of how he's with us even in our doubts. Confronted with the historical fact that Jesus had been crucified, these disciples said: "'We had hoped that he was the one who was going to redeem Israel'" (Luke 24:21). The irrefutable events that had just taken place forced them to reevaluate what they had previously believed.

Jesus didn't rebuke them for their lack of faith; rather, he opened up the Scriptures and gently guided them back to the truth.

> And beginning with Moses and all the Prophets, he explained to them what was said in all the Scriptures concerning himself.
>
> As they approached the village to which they were going, Jesus acted as if he were going farther. But they urged him strongly, "Stay with us, for it is nearly evening; the day is almost over." So he went in to stay with them.
>
> When he was at the table with them, he took bread, gave thanks, broke it and began to give it to them. Then their eyes were opened and they recognized him, and he disappeared from their sight (Luke 24:27-31).

We don't know exactly how "their eyes were opened," but we know it was a spiritual awakening. God uses different means to address our doubts; but revelation from God, in all its forms, is always part of the equation.

God can also use argumentation and evidence. Jesus, in effect, *made a case* to these disciples. He presented the detailed textual evidence, and then, presumably, he reached out his hands to break the bread and revealed the *physical* evidence—the nail prints in his hands.

As we journey down the river (or the road) of doubt, we need to be looking and listening for every scrap of revelation God gives us. He's not stingy with himself, but he's always looking for a heart that's open and ready to receive his presence. That can be a doubting heart—but it must be a sincere and obedient heart as well. It must be a heart that "urges him strongly" to "stay with us." Whether we're facing doubts about ourselves, about others, or about the very nature of reality, we need our Creator to come alongside and join us on the road.

Summing-Up: Teddy Roosevelt explored the uncharted River of Doubt in South America—and that's a good metaphor for how we navigate through life. Doubt is not just normal; it's also necessary. Our lives are filled with questions about ourselves, others, and the nature of the world. These doubts can be productive when they lead us to growth and discovery.

For Further Reflection

1. Describe your journey on the River of Doubt. What are some of the obstacles you've had to face? What does the scenery look like?

2. In what ways has self-doubt played a positive role in your life?

3. Have you ever had suspicions about a person's character or motives without being able to put your finger on it? What happened?

4. If Jesus were to join you on the Road to Emmaus, what would you ask him? What doubts would you like for him to resolve?

CHAPTER 3

In Herod's Prison

Key Idea: We can doubt without
sinning as long as our doubts
bring us back to Christ.

HAVE YOU EVER DOUBTED what God is doing in your life? If so, then you're in good company. Most, if not all, the great saints of church history have struggled with doubts and fears. Many have even wondered at times if God had abandoned them altogether. Most of the great heroes of the Bible were likewise prone to question the goodness and presence of God.

Perhaps the most unexpected doubter of all is John the Baptist. He was described by Jesus as the greatest man born of women (Luke 7:28), and yet he faced a serious crisis of doubt toward the end of his life. John had fulfilled the calling of God. He had gone out on a limb. He had stood by the banks of the Jordan and in one bold declaration forever tied his ministry to an unknown and untested man from Nazareth.

But those heady days by the Jordan were now long past. John still had his inner circle of disciples, but the crowds were now following the one John had described as "'the Lamb of God, who takes away the sin of the world'" (John 1:29). John always knew this was part of the divine plan. "'He must become greater,'" he said. "'I must become less'" (John 3:30). He knew he was the forerunner to Christ, the "voice crying in the wilderness," the one preparing the way for the Messiah.

John had no doubts about his calling. It wasn't the planned obsolescence of

John the Baptist experienced doubt.

his ministry that bothered him, but rather the fear that he might have been wrong all along. Nothing was playing out the way he expected. The Kingdom of God seemed as remote as ever—and the kingdom of Herod was still firmly in place. John had publicly denounced Herod's adultery, and this had landed him in jail.

While he was imprisoned, John continued to follow the ministry of Jesus as closely as he could. No doubt he was waiting for the great unveiling of the messianic plan—just in time to spring John from the dungeon and restore the throne of David. Yet when day after day passed and the plan remained unfulfilled, John sent a message asking if Jesus was the Messiah or whether he should keep looking for another.

> This news about Jesus spread throughout Judea and the surrounding country.
>
> John's disciples told him about all these things. Calling two of them, he sent them to the Lord to ask, "Are you the one who was to come, or should we expect someone else?" (Luke 7:17-19).

What an amazing thing for John to ask! Was he really in doubt? A simple, straightforward reading of the biblical text leads to a clear answer: *Yes, John the Baptist experienced doubt.*

But not all Bible commentators agree. Some go to great lengths to clear John's reputation. J.C. Ryle, the Anglican bishop of Liverpool and a leading nineteenth-century evangelical, could not accept the possibility that John doubted Christ.

> Some think that John sent this message at a time when his faith was failing. They think that like many other saints in the Bible, he had his moments of weakness, and that his imprisonment, together with the fact that our Lord did nothing to deliver him, had made him begin to doubt whether Jesus was the Messiah. This explanation was maintained by Tertullian, but it is not satisfactory.

So what is a satisfactory explanation according to Ryle?

> John's message was not sent on his account, but on account of his disciples. It was not sent because his own faith was failing, but

because he wished those he was about to leave behind him to believe in Jesus as Messiah. One argument in favor of this view is the great improbability that one so eminently taught of God as John was, and so singularly clear in his past testimony, would forget his first faith and doubt whether Jesus was the Christ.

In a similar way, the editors of the standard evangelical commentary popularly known as *Jamieson-Fausset-Brown,* try to work around the text, even while asserting that they are just following a "simple and natural" interpretation.

Was this a question of doubt as to the Messiahship of his Lord, as Rationalists are fain to represent it? Impossible, from all we know of him. Was it then purely for the satisfaction of his disciples, as some expositors [such as Ryle], more concerned for the Baptist's reputation than for simple and natural interpretation, take it?

The commentary goes on to argue that John was impatient, not doubtful, as though there's a lot of difference between these two positions of the heart. Impatience is often one of the faces that doubt wears.

You'll engage in these kinds of exegetical gymnastics only if you think doubting is a sin. The plain reading of the text, however, is clear. *John doubted.* And when we put that fact squarely beside Jesus' evaluation of John, then we have the best evidence yet that it is not a sin to doubt. If we try to explain John's doubt away, however, then we've missed an important truth. Even this greatest man born of women weighed alternative explanations. Out of the

> *We have a natural tendency to ask questions and wonder why.*

circumstances of his life, he doubted. And Jesus didn't take those doubts as a personal affront but as an opportunity to remind John to embrace the truth he already knew.

Lessons from Prison

What can John teach us about doubt?

First, *we doubt because we're human.* It's in our very makeup; it's a part of what old writers used to call "our constitution." John the Baptist, as Jesus said, was the greatest man *born of women.* Jesus has given us the simplest explanation for why John doubted. *He was made of dust.*

Second, *we doubt because we're helpless.* We're all in prison, like John. We have a natural tendency to ask questions and wonder why. But sometimes the constitution of our mind and the circumstances of our life conspire to undermine our faith. The helplessness we feel as circumstances overwhelm us can be a breeding ground for doubt. But desperation can also motivate great faith. How do we respond? Do we wallow in our helplessness? Or do we allow the desperate situations of our lives to drive us back to the truth? John took his doubts to Jesus.

Third, *we doubt because we're "hemmed in."* John's in prison; he can't see beyond the four walls of his cell. He's bound by the here and now. None of us can see beyond our immediate circumstances. We can never take in the whole landscape; the walls and bars keep getting in the way. Paul understood that life crowds us and sometimes narrows our vision to a sliver of light. Writing to the church at Corinth, he described his own constricted perspective: "For when we came into Macedonia, this body of ours had no rest, but we were harassed at every turn—conflicts on the outside, fears within" (2 Corinthians 7:5).

This is why we need a great vision of what lies beyond the four walls of our present condition. God's promises lift us out of the prison of the flesh and the dungeon of the world into the glorious freedom of God's ultimate purpose. As Paul said, "I consider that our present sufferings are not worth comparing with the glory that will be revealed in us. The creation waits in eager expectation for the sons of God to be revealed" (Romans 8:18-19).

The ancient Greek philosopher Plato introduced a memorable image to describe the human predicament. He pictured us—all of humanity—as prisoners in the dark tunnel of our own experience. We're shackled by the limitations of our senses. Plato's "Allegory of the Cave" is a powerful reminder of what it means to inhabit flesh and blood and bones. The material world is so real to us and so tangible that it appears *final* in its purpose. We're hemmed in by our materiality.

We're all in Herod's prison—every one of us. Even the greatest figures of church history pulled hard against the chains of their flesh. "What a wretched man I am!" Paul exclaimed. "Who will deliver me from this body of death?" (Romans 7:24).

Martin Luther felt very much as if he were in prison in 1527. It was the 10-year anniversary of the Ninety-Five Theses he had nailed to the church door in Wittenberg. But it was one of the most difficult years of his life. The man who had stood against the power of popes and kings was crumbling inside from despair and doubt. He struggled constantly with physical infirmities—headaches, kidney stones, arthritis, stomach maladies, infections, and chest pains. He thought he was going to die.

The most difficult part for Luther, though, was the intense and unrelenting bouts of depression. He confided in his close friend, Melanchthon, and described the spiritual toll his doubts were taking.

> I spent more than a week in death and hell. My entire body was in pain, and I still tremble. Completely abandoned by Christ, I labored under the vacillations and storms of desperation and blasphemy against God. But through the prayers of the saints God began to have mercy on me and pulled my soul from the inferno below.

By the end of the year, Luther was able to look back and see the goodness of God sustaining him. He wrote the words that we still sing today as a testimony of his faith, "A Mighty Fortress Is Our God." Faith sustains us through the prison of circumstance so that we can say with Paul, "But thanks be to God! He gives us the victory through our Lord Jesus Christ" (1 Corinthians 15:57).

Keep Your Eye on Esau

Let's pull another detail out of the story of John the Baptist. He was in *Herod's* prison—not Caesar's. This is significant because of the family that Herod represented. He came from the unfortunate family tree that went back to Esau. As we read our way through the Bible, we need to keep a close eye on Esau and his descendants. They're never up to any good.

Esau is best remembered for his monumental impulsiveness and short-sightedness. His younger twin brother, Jacob, tricked him into selling his birthright, and all it represented, for a hearty bowl of lentil stew (Genesis 25). But nothing, no matter how satisfying it seemed at the moment, was worth what Esau gave up. One's position as the firstborn in a Semitic family was not a privilege to barter away on a whim. Only a very foolish man would do this.

What did Esau give up? A double portion of his father's inheritance—just for starters. But among the descendants of Abraham, the firstborn status carried even greater significance than normal. The firstborn was the bearer of Yahweh's promise to the great patriarch Abraham, and you couldn't put a price tag on that. Esau forfeited the promise and blessing of an intimate relationship with the Creator of heaven and earth. Some bowl of stew!

Scripture teaches that it's not Esau's foolishness but his fleshliness that undid him. Yes, Jacob was clever and Esau was stupid. But we'd be wrong to reduce this to the story of a trickster, which is a common folklore motif among the world's cultures. Jacob saw the great spiritual value in the blessing and birthright, while Esau couldn't see past his growling stomach. Here's how the writer of Hebrews summarizes the lesson.

> Make every effort to live in peace with all men and to be holy; without holiness no one will see the Lord. See to it that no one misses the grace of God and that no bitter root grows up to cause trouble and defile many. See that no one is sexually immoral, or is godless like Esau, who for a single meal sold his inheritance rights as the oldest son (Hebrews 12:14-16).

Esau is mentioned here as an object lesson. He's a type or picture of the fleshly man, living for *now*, living for *here*, completely unmindful that God has an eternal purpose for his creation. The godless man is bound by his senses, hemmed in by the instincts of his flesh and blood.

Who were Esau's descendants? They were constant thorns in the side of God's people, Israel. One of Esau's grandsons, Amalek, was the father of a nomadic line—the Amalekites (Genesis 36:12)—who were the first to oppose and attack Israel after the exodus from Egypt (Exodus 17:8-16). Following the example of the writer of Hebrews, many Bible teachers see in this grandson of Esau a picture of the flesh. A.B. Simpson wrote that "Amalek was a type of the flesh. He was descended from Esau; and Esau represented the carnal nature." C.H. Macintosh agreed with this: "Amalek represents the hindrance to their walk with God through the wilderness...Amalek stands before us as a type of the flesh."

One particularly loathsome branch of the Amalekites was fathered by Agag, king of the Amalekites. Agag was the king spared by Saul in direct disobedience to God's command (1 Samuel 15:8). We don't hear much more about Agag and his descendants until the story of Esther. The evil advisor to King Ahasuerus, Haman, who plotted the destruction of God's people, is described as an Agagite (Esther 3:1). The flesh is always seeking the destruction of faith.

But the story of Esau's influence throughout Scripture doesn't end here. The Edomites were a people living on the southeastern border of Israel. They were descended from Esau's family, and they constantly opposed Israel even though they were closely related to them. The Edomites refused to help when Judah was taken captive, and they even rejoiced at the fall of Jerusalem. Obadiah's short prophecy was directed squarely at this ancient antagonist of Jacob: "But how Esau will be ransacked, his hidden treasure pillaged!" (Obadiah 6). Obadiah prophesied that the Edomites would be completely cut off—"everyone in Esau's mountains will be cut down in slaughter" and Esau "will be destroyed forever" (Obadiah 9).

We are most susceptible to doubt when the world weighs heavy on us.

Another term used in Scripture for Edom is Idumea, which describes the area southeast of the Dead Sea. This is the land of Edom, so the Idumeans are really just Edomites by another name. This matters because Herod was an Idumean, the last of a line of Idumean rulers whose ancestry was ultimately traced back to Esau. Scripture is consistent with the symbolism: Esau's family is a picture of the flesh.

So what's the significance of Herod's prison? The flesh is the most ancient antagonist of faith. We are most susceptible to doubt when the world weighs heavy on us. Sometimes it seems as though the very chemistry of our body is pulling us toward the dust. This, then, is what Herod's prison represents symbolically—being bound in the flesh, imprisoned by our senses. John shows us that no one is exempt from this basic reason for doubting.

Shaken But Not Broken

It's a mystery to me why the same set of circumstances can lead one man to faith and another to unbelief. One can sit in prison and curse God, while another draws closer to God in worship. Aleksandr Solzhenitsyn could look out of Stalin's prison, out of the ferocious materiality of his life, and find faith.

In a prison yard in Siberia, the simple physical act of breathing drew him closer to God despite being hemmed in, mercilessly, by the world.

> There was rain in the night, clouds are drifting over the sky, and there is still an occasional sprinkle. I stand under an apple tree that is losing its blossom—and I breathe. The apple tree and the grass around it are saturated with moisture, and there is no name for the sweet and heady smell that intoxicates the air. I draw it deep, deep into my lungs, my whole chest tingles with the fragrance...So what if it is only a tiny garden hemmed in by five-storied buildings like cages in a zoo? I no longer hear the backfiring motorcycles, the howling radiograms, the crackling loudspeakers. So long as I can stand under an apple tree after rain and just breathe—it is possible to live.

The fresh smell of apple blossoms after rain was enough, even in the hellhole of Stalin's prison, to bring Solzhenitsyn back to God. Even when surrounded by deprivation, in "a tiny garden hemmed in" by concrete cages, the goodness of God can be felt, experienced, and acknowledged. And this is one of the most basic ways we worship our Creator. We give back to him hearts that gladly receive his goodness.

> Every good and perfect gift is from above, coming down from the Father of the heavenly lights, who does not change like shifting shadows. He chose to give us birth through the word of truth, that we might be a kind of firstfruits of all he created (James 1:17-18).

We breathe in with joy and thankfulness even the "little" that he gives. Faith takes what is little and realizes how great it really is—it's a down payment on some "very great and precious promises" (2 Peter 1:4). We're in prison right now, but we know that we "will receive a rich welcome into the eternal kingdom of our Lord and Savior Jesus Christ" (2 Peter 1:11).

"It is possible to live," Solzhenitsyn wrote. But not just live, as though living were ever its own end. We were made to live for someone and for some purpose greater than anything that Stalin or Herod could ever hold in prison. "'I have come that they may have life,'" Jesus said, "'and have it to the full'" (John 10:10).

Early in his career, Solzhenitsyn elaborated on this great truth in a short, private poem he wrote down as a prayer. He had no intention of publishing the poem, but one of his helpers released it without his permission. Solzhenitsyn's faith, and the kind of life that "it is possible to live," come more clearly into focus in the simple lines he wrote. "How easy for me to live with you, Lord!" he wrote. "How easy to believe in you!" In the midst of persecution, when his mind "flagged in bewilderment," Solzhenitsyn acknowledged where his faith came from: "You send me the clarity to know that you exist." The poem ends with a simple affirmation that "not all paths of goodness should be barred."

Faith is the clarity to know despite what our circumstances are telling us.

John the Baptist knew this as well. His mind was "flagging in bewilderment," as Solzhenitsyn put it. But the path to Christ was always open; "not all paths of goodness" were "barred." John couldn't take that path himself, so he sent two of his disciples instead with a message.

> When the men came to Jesus, they said, "John the Baptist sent us to you to ask, 'Are you the one who was to come, or should we expect someone else?'"
>
> At that very time Jesus cured many who had diseases, sicknesses and evil spirits, and gave sight to many who were blind. So he replied to the messengers, "Go back and report to John what you have seen and heard: The blind receive sight, the lame walk, those who have leprosy are cured, the deaf hear, the dead are raised, and the good news is preached to the poor" (Luke 7:20-22).

We should note several key things about John's question and the unusual answer that Jesus gives.

First, John doesn't make an accusation that is anchored in himself or his conditions. He is asking for a clarification, for a fuller revelation of who Christ is. He is asking for "the clarity to know," as Solzhenitsyn prayed. Doubt is fuzzy thinking and fogged-up windows. Faith is the clarity to know despite what our circumstances are telling us.

John might have started by saying, "Why haven't you rescued me from jail if you're really the Messiah?" He could have made his own sorry condition the foundation of his approach to Christ. But he didn't do this. His question was motivated by circumstances he didn't understand, but he didn't dwell on himself. He sought to understand Christ better. When I dwell on *my* questions and *my* circumstances, doubt is holding me in bondage to *myself.* That's where faith steps in and draws me out beyond myself toward God.

Second, Jesus didn't answer directly but continued what he was already doing. "*At that very time,*" Luke says, "Jesus cured many who had diseases." He didn't take offense at John's question. He didn't say, "I can't believe that John, *of all people,* is asking that!" As Jesus continued healing the sick and giving sight to the blind, he sent back the message. "Look at what I'm doing *right now.*"

When we judge God according to the narrow criteria of our own to-do list, it can seem that he is sitting on his hands. But God is constantly at work; he is constantly sustaining us. God never stops bringing his good purpose to completion both in ourselves and in his creation. We overcome doubt when we begin to see what God is doing right now.

Third, Jesus reminded John of what he already knew. As he continued healing the sick, Jesus fulfilled the prophecies spoken many centuries before about the Messiah. Jesus was drawing John's attention back to the promises of God.

Isaiah had prophesied that when Messiah comes, "the eyes of the blind shall be opened, and the ears of the deaf unstopped" (Isaiah 35:5 ESV). The prophecy is repeated throughout Isaiah, and John would have understood what Jesus was speaking about. Opening the eyes of the blind, in particular, came as close as anything to being the Messiah's calling card.

But Isaiah said much more—and John would have been thinking of this too. A few chapters later, after mentioning once again that the Messiah would "open eyes that are blind," Isaiah then adds that he would "free captives from prison" and "release from the dungeon those who sit in darkness" (Isaiah 42:7). This must have been what John was expecting from the Messiah. After all, Isaiah could have been describing *him,* sitting in the darkness of Herod's dungeon. But on this point, Jesus left him hanging. He didn't address that part of the messianic prophecy at all. There were still some things that John had to take on faith, even if he didn't fully understand.

The ultimate purpose of Christ's mission was to free us from sin—to bring us out of the dungeon of spiritual death. We're all sitting in Plato's cave, sitting in darkness, bound by our flesh. Christ descended into our dungeon and became like us, so that when he ascended, he could lead "captives in his train" and give "gifts to men" (Ephesians 4:8). For a moment, even John couldn't see beyond the prison walls to the fulfillment of his own prophecy. "'Look, the Lamb of God,'" he once said, pointing to Jesus, "'who takes away the sin of the world'" (John 1:29). Jesus sent back a partial answer to John, because John already knew the rest. He knew what God had promised. He just needed to accept again by faith what his eyes could not see.

> *We have an advocate when we struggle in our faith. Christ defends our reputation in the courtroom of heaven.*

After John's disciples left, Jesus turned to the crowd. He knew they were probably confused about everything they had just witnessed.

> "What did you go out into the desert to see? A reed swayed by the wind? If not, what did you go to see? A man dressed in fine clothes? No, those who wear expensive clothes and indulge in luxury are in palaces. But what did you go out to see? A prophet? Yes, I tell you, and more than a prophet. This is the one about whom it is written:
> 'I will send my messenger ahead of you,
>   who will prepare your way before you.'
> I tell you, among those born of women there is no one greater than John" (Luke 7:24-28).

I like how Jesus sticks up for John here. We too have an advocate when we struggle in our faith. Christ defends our reputation in the courtroom of heaven. We know this because he's always interceding for us and always pleading our case (Romans 8:34). He defends us against our accuser, Satan (Revelation 12:10-11).

We also know this because of what Jesus said next. After declaring that John was the greatest "'among those born of women,'" he says, "'yet the one who is least in the kingdom of God is greater than he'" (Luke 7:28).

That means there's hope for you and me too. We have no greatness in ourselves; but God sees the greatness of his unfolding, and eternal, work of salvation. He sees our faith as we wait like John in prison, as we wait like creation itself, to be "delivered from the bondage of corruption into the glorious liberty of the children of God" (Romans 8:21 NKJV).

Summing-Up: Even John the Baptist experienced doubt when he was imprisoned by Herod. In a sense, we're all in prison—bound by the flesh, shackled by our senses. Our flesh pulls us toward doubt. The example of John, however, shows that our doubts can lead us back to Christ. Our doubts can be the grounds upon which a vibrant faith is reaffirmed.

For Further Reflection

1. When are you most vulnerable to doubts? Is there a time of the day or a season of the year when doubts come more readily to you?

2. What kind of circumstances or people can become the "Herod" in your life?

3. Are you hesitant to bring your doubts to God? How do you expect him to respond when you do this?

4. Read 1 Samuel 30:1-6 and Acts 16:22-28. How did David and Paul respond to their circumstances? How can their examples help you deal with doubt?

Chapter 4

The Boy with the Cigarette

Key Idea: Doubt is a lot like
temptation and should be faced
by following Jesus' example.

IT WAS TABOO. IT WAS FORBIDDEN. It was also disgusting.

I'd plucked the cigarette from the sidewalk where it lay unsmoked, having fallen from the fingers or pocket of a passerby—a little white cylinder of potential sin.

I picked it up.

Where I got the matches, I don't remember. But it was a premeditated act of rebellion.

My father figured it out the minute I walked through the door. The sour smell of cigarette smoke hung around me like a cloud. After lecturing me sternly, he gave me my punishment, which was surprisingly lenient, I thought. I was to write out a verse, 1 Corinthians 10:13, enough times to remember it. I can still quote it perfectly in the King James Version.

> There hath no temptation taken you but such as is common to man: but God is faithful, who will not suffer you to be tempted above that ye are able; but will with the temptation also make a way to escape, that ye may be able to bear it.

Doubt is not sin, but it certainly looks a lot like temptation. The connection is real, and I don't want to downplay its significance. It would be a mistake to normalize doubt to such an extent that we remove every stigma, ignore every pitfall, and dismiss every danger. A warning sign should be posted before every question we ask: *Doubt at Your Own Risk.*

Yes, doubting is normal, but so is temptation—and temptation, as we know from experience, is nothing to take lightly. To be sure, even temptation can lead to spiritual growth in the same way that resistance makes a tree stronger. Our resolve to follow Christ is strengthened with each denial of the flesh. Every rejection of worldly pleasure brings the joys of heaven more clearly into focus.

> *Doubt is not sin, but it certainly looks a lot like temptation.*

But still, if I had my druthers, I would rather not be tempted at all. And I would choose not to doubt. That's not an option, though, as long as we're in this flesh. So instead, we need to find productive ways to handle every challenge to our faith. We can start by considering how much alike doubt and temptation really are.

Common to Man

How is doubt like temptation? One way is that it takes me, sneaks up on me, lays a firm hand on my shoulder and turns me around. I no longer seem to be in control of myself. I've been taken when I wasn't watching. We can do our best to avoid temptation—to "flee youthful lusts" (2 Timothy 2:22 NKJV) and to "not give the devil a foothold" (Ephesians 4:27). But we can't avoid temptation altogether, since it's lodged within our flesh.

And this is true of doubt too.

When we dig into the Greek word for "take," we find a fairly innocuous word, *lambano*, with a wide range of functional meanings that fall along the spectrum of "taking" and "receiving." In certain contexts, as in 1 Corinthians 10:13, the word can carry a stronger sense of overtaking and seizing. Jerome's Latin translation, the Vulgate, is helpful here, since Jerome lived a whole lot closer (fifth century AD) to the living Greek of the New Testament than we do. Jerome chose the Latin word for "apprehend" to capture the sense of what Paul is saying. Doubt, like temptation, *apprehends* us. We never have to pursue doubts in order to experience them. They come upon us suddenly and stop us in our tracks.

But there's another dimension to the Greek word that suggests the reciprocal act of *receiving*. Temptation comes upon us, and we can't avoid it. We *are* tempted—in the fullest, passive sense of that verb. Doubt is like this too. We question—but we *are* questioned as well. Doubt puts us under the bright lights and subjects us to an interrogation of our faith. None of this is very pleasant, and none of it can be avoided.

> *Doubt puts us under the bright lights and subjects us to an interrogation of our faith.*

There's a third similarity. Doubt and temptation are both ordinary experiences. They are "common to man." We use three words in English to capture a single adjective in Greek, *anthropinos*. The whole suite of human experience is bound up in that word. Doubt is part of the package of our humanity.

Still another similarity is that doubt and temptation both provide opportunities for either victory or defeat. In both cases, we are weighing choices—which brings us back to our working definition of doubt, "the consideration of alternatives." Shall I believe God or shall I believe this serpent who is questioning God (Genesis 3:4-5)? Behind original sin there's an original temptation; go behind the temptation and you'll find an original doubt. We shouldn't forget this connection between doubt and temptation. Doubting always comes with risks.

So how do we handle the boy with the cigarette? My dad was firm, but he administered grace. How does the church handle those loitering on the edges of doubt? Three strategies have defined the church's approach to doubt—ignoring, refuting, and embracing it. I'm going to describe these as the *way of the ostrich,* the *way of the hawk,* and the *way of the cuckoo.* As we look at each of these, we should keep in mind the close connection between doubt and temptation. We'll come back to this at the end when we look at how Jesus handled the temptation he faced.

The Way of the Ostrich

I'm not sure I've ever heard a sermon on doubt, though a few Easter messages on Doubting Thomas come to mind. Thomas is our go-to guy when the subject comes up. But that's just it. The subject *doesn't* come up very often, and not because the Bible doesn't have much to say. We just don't want to talk about it. We choose to ignore it. We choose the way of the ostrich.

One of the ways we do this is to submerge doubt—to bury it beneath creeds, legalistic rules, and formalism. Alfred Lord Tennyson, poet laureate of England during the reign of Queen Victoria, put his finger on the strategy.

> There lives more faith in honest doubt,
> Believe me, than in half the creeds.

Faith in Christ doesn't sweep away all our questions.

To the extent that creeds are shortcuts to faith, roundabouts that discourage theological reflection, they do faith a great disservice. Creeds and catechisms serve a valuable role in the life of the church; but the faithful must be taught to reflect upon the statements, to ponder the logical interactions of the clauses—and not just mindlessly affirm a fossilized set of propositions.

Another way we ignore doubt is to stigmatize it. To many Christians, doubt is a taboo—something not to touch or even talk about. Taboos set boundaries around the natural, physical, earthy aspects of our lives, such as sexual behavior, excretory functions, and death. Doubt fits right in here since it grows out of the soil of our flesh. *We doubt because we're made of dust.*

This is very confusing to the young believer who is finding out that faith in Christ doesn't sweep away all our questions and that not too many people in the church are ready to help us with the broom anyway. Young believers have many questions, but all too often they hear "Just believe!" as though we can casually set our questions aside.

The nature of our minds, however, is to be constantly searching, always reaching for a settled point. Like water that is always flowing down to a draw, some place where the water pools and rests, our minds too have a gravitational pull toward *sense-making*. It's a basic law of human nature. We will continue to ask questions whether we want to or not.

Taboos lead us to speak in euphemisms, roundabout ways of referring to these bodily things we'd rather not discuss in polite company. We say things like, "Take the next exit, Joe, because I've got to use the bathroom," or "Aunt Hazel passed away last night." In a similar way, we speak of challenges and difficulties, we talk of tests and struggles. But we seldom bring ourselves to say, "What I'm feeling right now is *doubt*."

We should be able to face these subjects in a normal, healthy, and balanced way without denying their reality. If we treat doubt as an unspoken taboo, like leprosy in the Old Testament that must be put outside the camp, then we set Christians up for tragic failure. Why? Because doubt is *anthropinos*—it's "common to man." Christians should be encouraged to discuss their doubts, in biblical ways and in appropriate contexts, without fear or shame.

Friedrich Nietzsche, who was both the son of a Lutheran pastor and a passionately anti-Christian philosopher, identified this tendency to stigmatize doubt. "Christianity has done its utmost," he wrote, "to close the circle and declared even doubt to be sin." In his usually one-sided and hostile way, Nietzsche painted Christianity as the enemy of inquiry and progress. This remains the party line of a new generation of atheists. Indeed, many of the testimonies of skeptics are cast as stories of liberation and freedom from the social pressures of this taboo within the church. Unfortunately, the church does bear some blame for refusing to handle doubt in a way that's both healthy and biblical.

Still, we shouldn't let Nietzsche lecture us on doubt. But neither should we miss the point he's making. He hits too close to the mark. The notion that "doubt is sin" is seldom expressed so nakedly, but it's lurking behind much of our sermonizing and posturing on faith. The pews are full of closeted doubters. I've been asked to pray for sickness, financial problems, anxieties, insomnia, depression, and struggles with temptation. But I've never been asked to pray for someone's doubts. Parents have brought their children's doubts to me for prayer—but never their own. Why?

That's how deep the stigma runs. Charles Spurgeon understood this. The great Victorian preacher was given to fits of depression. His private journals reveal a great man of God who struggled with internal fears and doubts. Most of Spurgeon's contemporaries had no idea what was going on inside the preacher as he proclaimed God's Word with power and confidence. One time, however, he pulled back the veil a little and let his congregation know that he too was a man who struggled.

> I once told my congregation that I had passed through a season of doubt and fear. One of my elders said to me, "Sir, I am sorry you told the people that. Just suppose you had been swearing or stealing, you would not have told them of it?" No, I answered:

that would be a terrible thing. "Well," he replied, "I don't think it is much worse than not believing God; and, if you go and tell the people that, you are a bad example."

If Spurgeon had merely said, "I've faced some challenges and testings of my faith," he would have been viewed as a saint. But admitting to doubt gave him feet of clay. Of course, there are practical limits to what we should divulge to others. We shouldn't be transparent panes of glass. But there's a real danger too in hiding our humanity. The elders of the Metropolitan Tabernacle believed that it was preferable for Spurgeon to ignore his doubt than to be authentic before his congregation. Spurgeon's instincts were better than that.

The Way of the Hawk

Christianity has always encouraged a robust tradition of apologetics. We defend our faith because we believe it's *true*. Our faith is unavoidably connected to historical claims, and this all but requires that we provide *reasons* for why we believe. We believe in the historical reality of Abraham's call. We believe that God actually delivered Israel from Egypt. We believe that David, the ancestor of Jesus, was a real person who lived and reigned in ancient Israel. These historical claims matter because they are the foundation for every historical claim the Bible makes about Christ.

We believe that Jesus was a real person who was born of a virgin in Bethlehem. We believe he really claimed to be the Son of God. We believe he knew his death was a sacrificial atonement for sins—not that this was a theological claim made up about him later by the apostle Paul. We believe he rose again from the dead and ascended back to heaven. And because of this, we believe him when he said he's coming back someday.

Paul acknowledged the importance of history to our faith. He lists all the reasons why we can be confident that Christ actually rose from the dead (1 Corinthians 15:3-8), and then he makes an amazing statement: "If only for this life we have hope in Christ, we are to be pitied more than all men" (1 Corinthians 15:19).

These claims make up the nonnegotiable core of orthodox Christianity. We affirm certain things to be historically true. But what I'm describing as *the way of the hawk* takes us in a little different direction. The hawk hovers over the field, looking for the stray rabbit or mouse, ready to swoop down on the easy prey. The hawk as apologist takes the battle to the enemy, clears the field, and does so with impressive speed and skill. Logic and argumentation are brought to the fields of doubt, and the prey is picked off one by one. *Where did Cain get his wife?* The hawk is ready to dive down and sink its talons into the helpless victim.

> *The church's greatest theologians have produced an impressive edifice of logical argumentation, and yet many still turn away in unbelief.*

But the hawk doesn't just pick off isolated problems one by one. The hawk surveys the field and seeks to bring the really big questions under its control too—the worldview questions about the existence of God, the reliability of Scripture, and the problem of evil. The hawk seeks to impose a rational, orderly mastery over the entire landscape.

There's real value in the work of the hawk. We need to know there are answers. We need to know that our faith is intellectually coherent. But the hawk doesn't make the field safe for faith. The church's greatest theologians and philosophers have produced an impressive edifice of logical argumentation, and yet many still turn away in unbelief.

One of the church's great hawks was the medieval philosopher Anselm of Canterbury, who constructed the famous ontological proof for the existence of God (which is too involved to go into here). Philosophers find Anselm's argument elegant, attractive, and even persuasive. And yet most philosophers don't believe in God. You see, the problem is that logic is not the ultimate answer to doubt because doubt isn't just a matter of the mind; it's an affair of the heart.

The early twentieth century witnessed a resurgence of hawks in the church. Traditional Christian faith had reached a crisis point with the combined onslaught of Darwinian theory and German historical skepticism, the so-called "higher criticism." The fundamentalist movement was rightly motivated to combat the skepticism and liberalism that were seeping into the church. Fundamentalism sought to bolster faith against the advancing claims of science and the skeptical dissection of the Bible—and it attempted to do so with logic, argumentation, and evidence. Doubt was battled systematically, question by question. The "certain" findings of science and the "certain" findings of higher criticism were confronted with the certain dogmatism of fundamentalism.

But what happens when you weigh the evidence and your doubts remain? Do you not have enough faith? Is there something wrong with you? The hawk doesn't have a good answer for that. The hawk may have very sharp eyesight, but he fails to see the humanity of doubt. The defense of dogma became dogmatism—and dogmatism has little patience with those who doubt.

> *Our faith has to rest on something other than good arguments and nimble logic.*

Christians have always struggled, it seems, to find a balance between the bold proclamation of truth and the gracious understanding of doubt. Jude told us "to contend for the faith that was once for all entrusted to the saints" (Jude 3); but at the end of this short letter, Jude also told us to "be merciful to those who doubt" (v. 22). We are to defend the truth aggressively, but to do so consistent with the liberty and grace we have in Christ.

The best of the fundamentalist legacy is a robust defense of the coherence and reliability of the Bible and the cardinal doctrines of the Christian faith. The worst legacy, however, is a stifling ignorance—a reluctance to inquire, a rigidity about nonessentials. The best apologetics are sustained reflections on truth. The worst offer executive summaries, predigested talking points, and rhetorical zingers, all of which misunderstand and trivialize doubt.

Hawks should reflect on this sobering thought: Muslims have their own hawks, as do Mormons and even atheists. So our faith has to rest on something other than good arguments and nimble logic.

The Way of the Cuckoo

A third way to deal with doubt is to embrace it. This starts with viewing it no longer as a stigma (which is good), then granting it a certain mystique (which is unfortunate), and finally incorporating it into our worship (which is wrong). Franz Kafka told a strange little parable about how we turn the oddest things—often the things we can't control, such as doubt—into rituals.

> Leopards break into the temple and drink to the dregs what is
> in the sacrificial pitchers; this is repeated over and over again;

finally, it can be calculated in advance, and it becomes a part of the ceremony.

This is an apt description of how postmodern Christians today seek to normalize doubt to the point of celebrating it, making it "part of the ceremony."

The intellectual fashion of our day is to embrace uncertainty, and Christians who do this are trending with the post-

> *The intellectual fashion of our day is to embrace uncertainty, and Christians who do this are trending with the postmodern current.*

modern current. This is the way of the cuckoo. The cuckoo bird lays its egg in somebody else's nest. It then flies away and lets the unsuspecting host incubate its eggs and raise its children.

Whole sectors of the evangelical church are following the way of the cuckoo. They've abandoned their nests and allowed the world to raise their young. These Christians have adopted postmodern uncertainty as the foundation of their faith. This is not only wrong, it's destructive of our faith. Our foundation is certain, and that certainty rests in who Jesus Christ is and what he has done. That has always been the secure starting point for our faith. We have no business placing our young in any other nest.

Those who promote an uncertain faith—a faith with fuzzy edges—display a dangerous love for the intellectual and cultural values of this world. The desire for intellectual respectability comes with a price. It's a seductive siren call. Like Odysseus, we might want to hear the sirens—to read and debate and enjoy the world's philosophical delicacies—without being drawn to destruction. We fail to see, however, that the world's philosophies are just as fleshly as bodily indulgences. They feed our flesh, and they encourage our instinct to doubt.

I know something about the lure of intellectual respectability. As a young man in graduate school, I walked away from my faith and found that I had to replace it with something else. My friends were artists and actors, writers and dancers. Art was becoming my religion.

During this time I cultivated a brief and nasty penchant for smoking unfiltered Gauloises cigarettes. The critical factor for me, as one who hated smoking, was that Gauloises were *French*—as French as Camus and Derrida and Foucault. The cigarette was known for being short, fat, unfiltered, with dark and pungent Turkish tobacco. It was the cigarette of choice for French intellectuals.

I couldn't stand the wretched little things, but they were a necessary part of the costume of the intelligentsia, and I was foolishly chasing a mystique. When you've figured out the world, and you're only 21, then you do things like this. For many postmodern Christians, doubt is the nasty little cigarette hanging from their lower lip.

Doubt as Sacrament

This is the natural progression to how the church has dealt with doubt. First, it's ignored. Then, when it just won't go away, we try to refute it. Finally, we decide to live with it and normalize it within the boundaries of our lives.

> *Doubt is neither a stigma nor a badge of honor. It's just one more opportunity to know God.*

How much better if we sanctify it and acknowledge that doubt is a natural part of how God made us. It's neither a stigma nor a badge of honor. It's just one more opportunity to know God, one more thing to sanctify to the one who made us.

How much better if we recognize the sacramental properties of doubt—that is, how it initiates us into the life of faith.

A sacrament is a ritual *with meaning*. It's a ritual of participation and identification, like baptism and communion. We identify with Christ just as he identified with us. Christ brought all of his humanity before the Father when he agonized in the Garden of Gethsemane. He was "tempted in every way, just as we are—yet was without sin" (Hebrews 4:15). The humanity of Christ would be a meaningless theological dogma if Jesus hadn't felt the weight of his material body pressing down upon his Spirit. Jesus asked *why?*—and so do we. We participate in his agony, but we must participate right through to the end. "'Yet not what I will,'" Jesus prayed to the Father, "'but what you will'" (Mark 14:36). Can we say that too in the midst of our questions and doubts?

Like everything else of this world, like everything that makes up the dust of our material existence, we should set the experience of doubt apart for God and his glory. This is what *sanctify* means—to take something out of the world's domain and commission it for God's service. Doubt, like suffering, is a tool God is able to use, if only we turn it over to him. When we sanctify doubt, we're letting doubt *sharpen our faith, not shake it.*

So how exactly do we sanctify doubt? We follow the pattern set by Jesus. We identify with him and reenact his victory. Scripture tells us that Jesus was tempted by Satan for 40 days in the wilderness.

> Jesus, full of the Holy Spirit, returned from the Jordan and was led by the Spirit in the desert, where for forty days he was tempted by the devil. He ate nothing during those days, and at the end of them he was hungry (Luke 4:1-2).

If doubt is like temptation, then we should learn from Jesus' example. Meaningful reenactment is the essence of a sacrament—so let's see what Christ did so that we can reenact his example in our lives.

First, we see that *Jesus answered doubt with the Word of God.* There's a positive affirmation here as well as a negative denial. When we answer doubt with God's Word, this means that we're *not* answering with better arguments but with the very breath of God.

> The tempter came to him and said, "If you are the Son of God, tell these stones to become bread."
>
> Jesus answered, "It is written: 'Man does not live on bread alone, but on every word that comes from the mouth of God'" (Matthew 4:3-4).

Jesus wasn't speaking here of the "words" of God, as though there's some magical property in the syllables we pronounce. Power is found in the *Word* of God, not the *words.* This is a subtle but crucial distinction. We can memorize words by storing them in the synapses of our brain, but we can hide God's Word only in our hearts (Psalm 119:11). In the language of the Bible, the heart is the seat of our will and emotion.

Notice that Jesus didn't say, "No, I'm not hungry." He didn't say, "I'm God and I don't need to eat." Jesus the Man answered in a way consistent with his humanity. He acknowledged his hunger; he recognized his human limitations. "Man does not live on bread alone." The word *alone* is easy to overlook, but it conveys an important truth. Yes, we do live by bread. We are physical beings as well as spiritual. God has designed us to be both, and both are essential to what God intends for us. We're not just spiritual beings who inhabit physical bodies for a time. God always intended for us to have a corporeal existence, which is why we'll someday have glorified *bodies* (Romans 8:23).

Yes, bread is necessary—but it's not enough. Jesus shows us that the gravitational pull of the dust can be overcome only by the pull of the Spirit. Jesus was "full of the Holy Spirit," just as Isaiah had prophesied (Isaiah 11:2). The life of the Spirit is the life of faith, and faith always comes by the Word of God (Romans 10:17). God's resources—faith, the Holy Spirit, the Word of God—are all bound together. This is our spiritual bread.

> *When we allow ourselves to become consumed by doubt, we're letting our questions drown out the voice of God.*

We shouldn't underestimate the importance of God's Word. It sustains us. It's God's very presence among us through the Spirit. When we allow ourselves to become consumed by doubt, we're letting our questions drown out the voice of God. We turn to books and experts; we read *about* God's Word instead of taking it into our soul. We're like a man dying of starvation who is desperately thumbing through cookbooks, looking at recipes and salivating over pictures, when a freshly baked loaf of bread is sitting on the table.

Elijah was like this. He doubted God, ran away into the wilderness, curled up into a ball, and fell asleep. An angel poked him and woke him up. The angel offered him something far greater than "answers." The angel offered him bread. And since Elijah was having a hard time hearing God through the noise of all his doubts, God turned up his hearing aid so that he could hear once again the "still small voice" of the Lord (1 Kings 19:9-12).

There's a second thing we learn from Jesus: *We must always remember the big picture.* Perhaps this is the hardest thing to remember when we doubt; but it's the most important. We were made for a purpose.

> The devil led him up to a high place and showed him in an instant all the kingdoms of the world. And he said to him, "I will give you all their authority and splendor, for it has been given to me,

and I can give it to anyone I want to. So if you worship me, it
will all be yours."

Jesus answered, "It is written: 'Worship the Lord your God
and serve him only'" (Luke 4:5-8).

This is what we were made for. Nothing else makes sense. When you
doubt, turn instead to God with an ambitious worship agenda. Ask God for
a greater vision of his glory as you worship him. Take every opportunity to
testify, speak, and witness of God's goodness and greatness—which is one of
the most basic ways we worship our Maker. When we do this, we're focusing on what we already know about God instead of dwelling on our doubts.

We should never throw away what we know for what we don't know. That's
always a bad bargain. Jack got magic beans when he bartered away the family cow,
but it doesn't work that way in the spiritual realm. God gives us what he wants
us to have. God tells us what he wants us to know. Yes, we should be ambitious:
we should wrestle as Jacob did and ask the Angel of the Lord for his ID (Genesis
32:29). But in the end, we must accept what God has chosen to reveal.

At the end of his long career, Moses reminded Israel that they were
responsible for what God had already revealed to them, not what God chose
to hold back: "The secret things belong to the LORD our God, but the things
revealed belong to us and to our children forever, that we may follow all the
words of this law" (Deuteronomy 29:29).

We can avoid a lot of grief if we keep this basic principle in mind. We want
to get behind the screen of Genesis 1 and understand the mechanism and
timetable of God's mighty acts. We want to reconcile the sovereignty of God
with the free will of man. We want every paradox of our faith and every apparent contradiction in Scripture to be resolved. But God says I'm account-
able for everything he's chosen to tell me, not what he's withheld. I am called
to be obedient to his will, and no question, doubt, or objection ever cancels
out that moral obligation.

Third, Jesus shows us that *we shouldn't try to outsmart our heavenly Father.*
We shouldn't try to trip God up, the way the scribes and Pharisees always tried
to do. We're not going to get anywhere doing that.

> The devil led him to Jerusalem and had him stand on the highest
> point of the temple. "If you are the Son of God," he said, "throw
> yourself down from here. For it is written:

'He will command his angels concerning you
   to guard you carefully;
they will lift you up in their hands,
   so that you will not strike your foot against a stone.'"
Jesus answered, "It says: 'Do not put the Lord your God to
the test'" (Luke 4:9-12).

It's normal and even necessary to doubt. We can't avoid it. But when we dwell on our doubts, when we relate to God only through our questions, then we're putting him to the test. We're standing on the roof of the temple daring God to come through for us. God is patient, but he can grow weary of our questions. "'Who is this,'" God asked Job, "'that darkens my counsel with words without knowledge?'" (Job 38:2).

> *When we dwell on our doubts, when we relate to God only through our questions, then we're putting him to the test.*

So how do we deal with doubt? Not by pretending it's not real or thinking that it can be conquered by our arguments. Not by absorbing it into the rituals of our life as something to be celebrated. We deal with doubt by participating in Christ's victory. Jesus has given us the pattern for how to triumph over the desires of the flesh, the illusions of the world, and the searchings of the mind—whether these come to us in the form of temptations or doubts.

Summing-Up: The church has often been guilty of responding to doubt in an unbiblical way—by stigmatizing, refuting, or celebrating it. Instead, we should follow Jesus' example when he was tempted. The experience of doubt should become an opportunity to identify with Christ and to reenact his victory over the flesh.

For Further Reflection

1. Which of the three approaches to doubt (the way of the ostrich, hawk, and cuckoo) do you identify with most? Why? What are the weaknesses of each approach?

2. How is it counterproductive to stigmatize doubt as a taboo? What would a healthy approach to doubt look like in the church?

3. Why are rational arguments not always sufficient to dispel our doubts?

4. As a man, did Jesus experience doubts as we do? How did his experience differ from ours? How was it similar?

CHAPTER 5

Asaph's Story

Key Idea: We can stop stumbling
over doubt and plant our feet again
in a stronger, more settled faith.

THE MOUNTAIN LAURELS WERE IN FULL, GLORIOUS BLOOM as I hiked back
down from the summit. Blossoms covered the wiry trees along the path—delicate white teacups with interiors etched in pink. At the height of its bloom,
the mountain laurel looks as though the finest miniature bone china has been
brought out for a doll party of innumerable guests.

Located along the Blue Ridge Parkway in Virginia, Sharp Top Mountain
was where I went to clear my head. It's a beautiful place, famous for its scenic
views and historical ghosts. Thomas Jefferson hiked this path in 1815 when
he was 72 years old. Robert E. Lee went there to experience the impressive
landscape. In 1943 a B-25 crashed into the summit, killing five airmen. The
wreckage is still littered along the side of the peak.

But for me, it was a place for thinking, reflecting, and praying. I would
clamber up a rock outcropping known as Buzzard's Roost and look out across
a green, manicured valley dotted with toy houses and farms. Overhead, hawks
would glide in the updraft. It was easy to be a child again.

The worst tumble I ever took came on Sharp Top. I was jogging back
down the path when I planted my foot on a loose rock. My foot slid and I
went down hard. My eyes were wide open the whole time, and so I watched

the world spin around me 360 degrees. No bones were broken, but I scraped and bruised myself pretty badly.

What happens when you slip? Your mind and body are suddenly and violently taken by surprise. Every muscle tightens and braces for the unknown. Your brain never had time to transmit a heads-up, so there's no preparation for what's coming next.

Doubt can take us like that, causing our spiritual and emotional muscles to tense up.

I fell hard that day on Sharp Top—but it could have been worse. Losing our footing can be comical, embarrassing, and sometimes painful. It can even be fatal. Consider what happened to Daniel and Rita—two tourists who ended up as tragic news items.

Daniel's dream had come true—a vacation on the magical Pacific island of Bali. He was 25 and enjoying the hike of his life, an early morning trek in the dense, luscious hills above the capital. The trail was advertised as safe, if a bit adventurous, since it took one to the rim of a volcano that has erupted some 26 times since 1840. But how often do you get the chance to peer down into the bowels of an active volcano? The rocks were slippery from a late-night rain, and as Daniel leaned over the edge into the abyss, he lost his footing. It took rescuers eight hours to retrieve his battered body from the rocks below.

Doubting is like falling, but it doesn't have to be fatal.

Rita too was a tourist on holiday from England with her husband, Keith. As she stepped out of the plane in Cancun, Mexico, the last thing on her mind, no doubt, was her own mortality. She emerged from the airplane and breathed in the heavy Gulf air. Rita enjoyed the warm touch of the sun for just a moment before her shoe caught on the steps. Keith watched helplessly as she tumbled down the metal steps onto the tarmac. He tried to shield her from the hot sun while waiting for the paramedics to arrive. But Rita was badly injured and bleeding profusely from the head. She died several days later in the hospital.

Doubting is like falling, but it doesn't have to be fatal. For all who have stumbled, for all who have planted their feet on loose rocks, the story of Asaph gives us hope.

The Doubter's Psalm

Asaph is a little-known doubter in the Bible. He's not as well-known as Thomas or Sarah, Elijah or John the Baptist; but in many ways Asaph has the corner on this subject. He is the doubter of record. *He wrote the book on doubt*—or at least he wrote a psalm about it.

We speak of "the psalms of David" as though he wrote them all. Actually, David wrote only about half the psalms. A lot of them are anonymous, and the rest were written by a handful of authors, including Asaph. So who was he?

Asaph was a worship leader during the reigns of David and Solomon, and he wrote 12 psalms—Psalm 50 and Psalms 73–83. He was a Levite, part of that family of priests who led Israel in sacrifice and worship. Asaph's reputation must have been considerable, since he was mentioned over 200 years after his death in the same breath as David: "King Hezekiah and his officials ordered the Levites to praise the LORD with the words of David and of Asaph the seer. So they sang praises with gladness and bowed their heads and worshiped" (2 Chronicles 29:30).

Asaph was much more than a worship leader. He spoke the very words of God. He was a prophet, a "seer"—one who sees into the future. We catch a hint of this in the first psalm attributed to him, Psalm 50.

> Our God comes and will not be silent;
> a fire devours before him,
> and around him a tempest rages.
> He summons the heavens above,
> and the earth, that he may judge his people:
> "Gather to me my consecrated ones,
> who made a covenant with me by sacrifice."
> And the heavens proclaim his righteousness,
> for God himself is judge. *Selah.*
> (Psalm 50:3-6)

This is a bracing apocalyptic vision—one that can be understood only with the Messiah squarely in view. When we read that "God himself is judge," we must remember that Jesus claimed that mantle of absolute authority for himself. Christ is the one who will "gather" the "consecrated ones." Christ is the one who will judge the living and the dead (John 5:25-30). There are

> *The apparent silence of God is one of the great mysteries that puzzle the faithful of every generation.*

even hints of the resurrection here in this gathering unto himself.

Asaph's words ring with certainty and confidence. He has no doubt that God will judge the wicked and set right the moral bearings of the earth. "Our God comes," Asaph declares, "and will not be silent" (v. 3). The apparent silence of God is one of the great mysteries that puzzle the faithful of every generation. Asaph was no exception. At the end of the psalm, God speaks to the wicked and denounces their evil deeds. And then God says, "These things you have done and I kept silent" (v. 21). God admits what we often suspect. *He chooses to be silent and let us wait.*

The apostle Paul understood that we can't be silent about the silence of God. "In the past God overlooked such ignorance, but now he commands all people everywhere to repent" (Acts 17:30). Paul is saying that God's silence *now* will be broken by a thundering judgment *some day.* Like Asaph, Paul was confident that God "has set a day when he will judge the world with justice" (Acts 17:31).

All of this is the backstory to the so-called "Doubter's Psalm." When we turn to Psalm 73, it's important to know what every ancient Jew would have known about Asaph. He was not some weak-in-the-knees novice. He was a man with a serious spiritual reputation.

Like a Radio Drama

Imagine for a moment that Psalm 73 is a radio drama from the 1930s. You gather around the radio at 8:00 p.m. and wait for your favorite show to come on. You know the main character well. He's a prophet, a musician, and a member of the king's inner circle. You've followed each episode that has shaped his life. Finally, the familiar theme music fills the room. An organ is laying down its heavy chord progressions and a baritone voice breaks in to enunciate: "And now we join Asaph's worship service already in progress."

> Surely God is good to Israel,
> to those who are pure in heart.
> (Psalm 73:1)

But then the tone shifts dramatically, and it's clear that we've entered the thoughts and feelings of the main character. Here's where the drama will unfold—in Asaph's heart and mind—and we'll know about it only because of the voice-over narration. You'd never know by listening to the trumpets, harps, lyres, cymbals, and tambourines (Psalm 150) that Asaph is struggling. You'd never know the battle that was raging inside his heart. We know this only because he tells us. The music fades out, and we hear an internal monologue that is very different from the public pronouncements of faith.

> But as for me, my feet had almost slipped;
> I had nearly lost my foothold.
>
> (v. 2)

Just like that, and we enter the interior world of a doubting believer. Asaph is talking to himself, which is a daring literary device to use in a worship song. The sudden shift disorients us. We nearly lose our footing too, just like Asaph. We're stunned by the candid revelation. Asaph was a seer, after all. He had *seen* things—seen and felt and experienced things only God could reveal. Not to mention, he had a reputation to maintain! Of all people, how could Asaph doubt? "But as for me," he says—which seems to place him outside the circle of those who are "pure in heart," those to whom God is good. "But as for me, my feet had almost slipped."

Almost, but not completely.

An Inside Job

Psalm 73 reveals the dark night of Asaph's soul. Charles Spurgeon, who knew a thing or two about doubt, described this psalm as "a great soul-battle, a spiritual Marathon, a hard and well-fought field, in which the half-defeated became in the end wholly victorious."

We should read the psalm as a detailed analysis of why we doubt—and how the believer ultimately redirects his doubt toward a renewed faith in God—because "everything that was written in the past was written to teach us" (Romans 15:4). Asaph shows us the ordinariness of doubt; but he also shows us what it takes to settle our feet once again on a solid foundation.

The Book of Psalms is a treasure house of God-revelation and gut-wrenching human experience, all jumbled together like the first two verses of Psalm 73. The loftiest expressions of divine majesty are often placed side by side with the deepest expressions of human failure. The psalmist is entrusted with the responsibility of bringing others into God's presence. And yet he's undergoing a crisis of faith. The world suddenly doesn't look the way it's supposed to—the way his own worship songs declare things to be.

The worst way to read a psalm such as this is to reduce it to an antiphonal chant in congregational worship. There's a place for this, and many of the psalms were intended for public recitation. Psalm 136, for example, is punctuated 26 times with the refrain, "His love endures forever." That just has to be read out loud.

> *I cannot doubt what*
> *I don't already believe.*

But many, if not most, of the psalms are much more private. They are interior echo chambers of worship, and it's best to slip into these psalms privately the way you might slide quietly into a pew in an empty cathedral. To chant these psalms as a congregation, especially when everybody is reading from a different translation, is to drain them of their inner vitality.

Psalm 73 is not a psalm to read aloud in public places. A psalm such as this has to be read from the inside out.

Here's where Asaph points us to a powerful truth: *Doubt is an inside job.* It always operates from within a belief system, not outside. If I doubt that "God is good to Israel," then it's only because I have already accepted this statement to be true. When I doubt, I'm not standing *outside* belief but *within* it. If I begin to doubt that the Bible is true, or that my sins are forgiven, or that Jesus is the Son of God, it's only because I've made a prior commitment to these truths. I cannot doubt what I don't already believe.

The power of this simple observation is often lost on us. We can view doubt as a foreign threat, an invasion force that's advancing against the walls of our faith; but doubt is actually right *here,* within the camp. That's why we should never silence our questions. They can provide valuable insights into how to keep the walls from getting breached by unbelief. Doubt is one of us—but he thinks like the enemy.

The implications of this are profound. First, this means that *doubt is evidence of faith.* Where there's smoke there's fire—and where there's doubt, there's going to be faith, no matter how weak or beaten down. Second, this means *we do have a choice.* We can give up, tear down the wall, and let the enemy in. Or we can "wake up" and "strengthen what remains and is about to die" (Revelation 3:2).

Ultimately, this is what Asaph did. He woke up. He saw the world clearly again from God's perspective. He strengthened what remained.

But not before he indulged in a few complaints against God.

Darwin's Deathbed

What unsettled the faith of Asaph? The question gnawing away at him is old and familiar, and it's not going away any time soon: *Why do the ungodly enjoy life so much? Why do they prosper while the righteous suffer?*

These questions cut right to the heart of our theology. If God is just and powerful, then why do we see so little of his justice in the world? And why does he seem so stingy with his power? Perhaps it's impertinent of us—the creature—to ask this of our Creator. But there's not a single one of us who hasn't wandered down this path. Asaph allows us to eavesdrop on his heart, so that we don't feel so bad about our own doubts.

> For I envied the arrogant
> when I saw the prosperity of the wicked.
> They have no struggles;
> their bodies are healthy and strong.
> They are free from the burdens common to man;
> they are not plagued by human ills.
> (Psalm 73:3-5)

Of course, Asaph is exaggerating. Everything looks distorted to him. He is choosing to see only one part of the equation—the momentary flourishing of the wicked. We're prone to this kind of selective vision; it's a childish habit we develop early when jockeying with our siblings. "You always let *her* get away with things!" we complain to Mom and Dad. "You treat *him* better than me!"

When we see the wicked "flourishing," our first instinct is to tell stories that explain these anomalies away. We want to iron out the wrinkles in God's justice. The true story, we believe, will set the record straight—and so we describe what *really* happened at Darwin's deathbed. We put words in the mouths of the dying that encourage the faithful and warn the infidel.

The Victorian era was a time of great doubt and skepticism when the claims of modern science seemed to go unanswered by the church. It was

> *We go to great lengths to deny what the Bible plainly says—that the godless sometimes live and die in relative peace and contentment.*

also a time that fostered a morbid interest in "final words." Books were written that catalogued the dying moments of history's illustrious men and women.

Christians picked up on the fashion and gave it an evangelical twist, focusing on the miserable deaths of the godless and the blessed passing of the godly. Deathbed conversion myths abounded in these stories, such as the fable told about Darwin's final days (which we'll get to shortly).

Asaph looked at the wicked, and they seemed to be dying as merry old men, quietly in their sleep after spending their entire lives filching from the poor and thumbing their noses at God. "There are no pangs in their death," he says (Psalm 73:4 NKJV).

We shake our heads like Asaph. It's almost as though we want to prove the Scripture wrong. *Psalm 73:4 can't be true,* we say, and we go to great lengths to deny what the Bible plainly says—that the godless sometimes live and die in relative peace and contentment.

Early in Christian history the story circulated in the church of how the pagan Roman emperor Julian the Apostate *really* died. Supposedly, he recanted his life of fierce opposition to Christ with this dramatic concession: "Thou hast conquered, O Galilean." There's very little evidence, however, that the story is true, no matter how vindicating it sounds to the ears of persecuted Christians.

The story about Darwin's deathbed is perhaps the best known example of how we try to revise Psalm 73:4 through cultural storytelling. In 1915 an article appeared in an obscure Baptist newsletter in the United States, the *Watchman Examiner,* claiming that Darwin had softened toward Christianity in his final days. The author was identified as a certain Lady Hope, a British evangelist who had lived a short distance from the home where Darwin died.

Lady Hope claimed to have visited Darwin during his final illness and found him reading the Bible—"which he was always studying." Though he specifically did not renounce his evolutionary views, Darwin did express regret to Lady Hope. "I was a young man with unformed ideas," he said. "People made a religion of them." And then he invited Lady Hope to speak to a small group of servants, tenants, and neighbors on his property. "What shall I speak about?" she asked, to which Darwin replied: "Christ Jesus and his salvation."

Darwin's children all emphatically denied the truth of the story. Many leading creationists have also recognized that it doesn't hold up to historical scrutiny. Still, the story circulates because we want to believe it—we want to believe that the godless come to their senses on their deathbeds and acknowledge the truth. We want, and we need, the vindication of our faith.

But we don't have to make up stories to handle our doubts. The Bible gives us a much surer refutation. Jesus told the story of a rich man who died in his riches (Luke 12:16-21); one of the things this story teaches is that the ungodly *do* prosper—but only for a time. God is patient, but God will surely judge the wicked.

What Went Wrong

The low point for Asaph, and the logical conclusion of his doubts, is that it's a vain thing to serve the Lord.

> Surely in vain have I kept my heart pure;
> in vain have I washed my hands in innocence.
>
> (Psalm 73:13)

If there is no justice in the world, if there is no goodness, if God must always remain silent, and if the godless die fat and happy, then we serve God in vain.

Job spoke at length about this. The prosperity of the wicked was a riddle that gnawed away at his soul.

> "Why do the wicked live on,
> growing old and increasing in power?
> They see their children established around them,
> their offspring before their eyes.
> Their homes are safe and free from fear;
> the rod of God is not upon them.
> Their bulls never fail to breed;
> their cows calve and do not miscarry.
> They send forth their children as a flock;
> their little ones dance about.
> They sing to the music of tambourine and harp;

they make merry to the sound of the flute.
They spend their years in prosperity
and go down to the grave in peace.
Yet they say to God, 'Leave us alone!
We have no desire to know your ways.'"
(Job 21:7-14)

Believers of every age have been brought to the edge of this thought—this terrifying thought: *What if it's not worth it in the end?*

Somehow, Asaph begins to snap out of it. He begins to realize a great truth—that his doubts didn't just sneak up on him unannounced. He lost his footing because he redirected his eyes. He took his eyes off the path. He was looking at the ungodly, and he saw something troubling. "This is what the wicked are like," he said in his despair. "Always carefree, they increase in wealth" (Psalm 73:12). The wicked were prosperous and happy. They died peaceful deaths. How could that be?

Something had gone wrong deep in his soul, at the depth of his being—the subflooring, if you will, of our humanity. The Greeks called this region of our being *nous*, the deep structure of consciousness on which all our intellectual faculties rest—judgment, the perception of the world, the awareness of good and evil, our capacity to know God and experience spiritual truth.

Our consciousness is the most basic thing God has given to us. It's what separates us from the animals; it's what allows me to know God and be known of God. Asaph's mind, his *nous*, has wandered. In the depth of his soul, he began to act and feel as though he were nothing but dust.

We can never avoid doubts altogether, but we can choose the things we dwell upon.

Asaph is describing the real human experience of daydreaming or mental wandering. His mind has veered off the path, and he's considering alternative explanations about the world. There's real danger here, because mental wandering is often closely related to moral wandering. That's why the Old Testament gives us so many admonitions to stay on the path and not turn "to the right or to the left."

> Make level paths for your feet
> and take only ways that are firm.
> Do not swerve to the right or to the left;
> keep your foot from evil.
>
> (Proverbs 4:26-27)

Here's the connection, once again, between doubt and temptation. We can never avoid doubts altogether; we can't avoid the "consideration of alternatives." Nevertheless, we are stewards and guardians of our thoughts. We can choose the things we dwell upon. We can choose what we feed our mind and where we direct our eyes.

> You will keep in perfect peace
> him whose mind is steadfast,
> because he trusts in you.
>
> (Isaiah 26:3)

> But his delight is in the law of the LORD,
> and on his law he meditates day and night.
>
> (Psalm 1:2)

> Let us fix our eyes on Jesus, the author and
> perfecter of our faith (Hebrews 12:1).

The imagery of staying on a level path—of "thinking in a straight line," as it were—is central to the Old Testament concept of the holy mind and the holy heart. This imagery lies behind the Hebrew word for repentance, *shûb*, which means to make a course correction, to leave the wrong path and get back onto the right path. When we indulge in daydreams, our mind is undisciplined and prone to doubt. We're most in danger of stumbling when we take our eyes off the path.

Here's the problem for us today. Thinking in a straight line is not viewed very highly. We value lateral thinking, creative thinking, nontraditional problem-solving, and thinking outside the box. It's essential, then, that we understand clearly what the Bible is describing to us. Moses delivered the commandment to "love the LORD your God with all your heart and with all your soul and with all your strength" (Deuteronomy 6:5). Jesus reaffirmed this commandment with a twist: "Jesus replied: 'Love the Lord your God with all your heart and with all your soul and with all your mind'" (Matthew 22:37).

We are to love him with our *minds*. And when you love someone or something, your mind is fixed on the object of your love. Neither Moses nor Jesus is advocating small-mindedness or closed-mindedness. They are commanding instead an unswerving commitment to what God has revealed. This should be a commitment that permeates every activity of the mind and body and leads to one thing—faithfulness.

The Big Turnaround

When we know we're falling, then we should find something, *anything,* to grab hold of. When my foot is slipping, I should find any toehold I can to stop the downward slide. I can build on that. I can climb up from any position I'm at, even if it's close to the bottom. This is what Asaph does. He stops falling. He plants his foot firmly on the smallest ledge of truth.

Two things keep Asaph from falling. First, *he remembers the community around him.* He recognizes his responsibility to others. What checks his heart is the effect his falling away would have on the community of faith. This is a remarkable thing to consider. Doubt affects other people. It's not just about me.

> If I had said, "I will speak thus,"
> I would have betrayed your children.
> (Psalm 73:15)

Asaph recognized the danger of spewing out the unfiltered feelings of his heart. What he expressed would matter to others. It would have consequences. Asaph knew that it's not enough to say, "I'm just being real," as though spilling our guts is its own justification.

Our culture tells me that it's not only my right but also an absolute necessity for sound mental health to express myself intimately, prolifically, and indiscriminately. I have more means at my disposal today to advertise my inner feelings and put my heart on public display. Blogs have institutionalized the social ritual of "writing about me." It used to be that nobody read someone's journal unless that person was famous and dead—a practice that's far preferable, I think, to the current promiscuity of thoughts and feelings. Asaph knows better than to become a stumbling block to others. He knows when to hold his tongue.

But Asaph remembers a second thing. *He remembers that he's more than dust.* He's more than a brute animal.

> I was senseless and ignorant;
>> I was a brute beast before you.
>
> (v. 22)

We'd express it a little differently today, probably using the language of artificial intelligence. We're not just computational machines. Our humanity cannot be reduced to binary code. There are atheists who proudly declare themselves to be robots, and yet they too love their children, who presumably are also robots.

Asaph will have none of this nonsense. He finds a place to plant his foot. It's a small ledge, but it's a great truth: *We are more than animals.* We are more than robots. We think and feel and love and doubt, and we can never fully grasp the wonder of all that we are. That's because we're made in the image of God. From that small ledge Asaph starts to climb again.

When we trust in God, there is benefit both now and for eternity.

In the end, Asaph has affirmed his faith by working through his doubt. He has owned up to his questions and acknowledged them. He has refused to deny and stigmatize what he genuinely felt; but neither does he ritualize and celebrate his doubt as some badge of authenticity. He reaches a triumphant ending. He acknowledges that when we trust in God, there is benefit both now and for eternity.

Asaph returns to the proper framework of worship, which is the affirmation of God's goodness. Doubt has not been denied or even refuted; the self has not been negated. But now the doubter is embracing God.

> Yet I am always with you;
>> you hold me by my right hand.
> You guide me with your counsel,
>> and afterward you will take me into glory.
> Whom have I in heaven but you?
>> And earth has nothing I desire besides you.
> My flesh and my heart may fail,
>> but God is the strength of my heart
>> and my portion forever.
>
> (vv. 23-26)

What had the ring of dead orthodoxy in the first verse is now validated as a personal faith.

> But as for me, it is good to be near God.
> I have made the Sovereign LORD my refuge;
> I will tell of all your deeds.
>
> (v. 28)

When we come back to the goodness of God, we've come back to faith. Only with eyes of faith can we believe that the same God who made all things good in the beginning (Genesis 1:31) will make all things good in the end (Philippians 1:6).

Summing-Up: Asaph was a worship leader and psalmwriter. He was also a believer whose faith was shaken by doubts. Asaph wondered why the wicked prosper and why God seems to be silent. "Is it worth it to serve God?" he wondered. Psalm 73 takes us on a remarkable journey from a faith that is stumbling, to a faith that becomes stronger than ever.

For Further Reflection

1. Have you ever stumbled badly? How was the physical act of stumbling like falling into doubt?

2. Asaph thinks of those who would be affected by his doubts. How responsible are we for the faith of others? (Read what Jesus said in Matthew 18:6-7.)

3. How can we be honest about our doubts without discouraging others who are weak in faith?

4. What specific things do we question about God and about the world when we see the wicked prospering?

CHAPTER 6

Windows in Heaven

Key Idea: There are good reasons
to believe even when our minds
can't fully understand.

THE YOUNG MAN LINGERED BEHIND after class a little longer than the other students who were already checking their voice mail and powering up their iPods and pushing through the double doors of the lecture hall.

"I was raised in a Christian home," he said. "But I don't believe in God anymore."

After his confession, Nate looked me in the eye to gauge my reaction. I'm not sure what he expected to see, but I didn't show surprise or condemnation. That's because I wasn't surprised. And I didn't condemn him. I understood, and I told him so.

Nate was polite and respectful. But I had said something in class that day about Darwin that he wanted to challenge. Darwin was really a pretext, though, for coming out and admitting his unbelief. He went on to describe for me what he'd been reading—a predictable list of skeptics and "former Christians."

I recognized Nate as the classic intellectual doubter. First, you start to doubt, and then you feed those doubts. And it never once occurs to you that you might as well choose to feed your faith instead.

Each year in my classes I see more and more young people like Nate who are "raised Christian" but get sucked into the vortex of a secular, rationalistic worldview. The heavens fall silent, and the only window that opens up is a

> *Material things are so solid, the senses are so alive, and God fades into a philosophical abstraction.*

window onto the world. Material things are so solid, the senses are so alive, and God fades into a philosophical abstraction.

When you're a young adult, doubt can easily get caught up in the mix of figuring out who you are and what you believe. Growing up is one of the most difficult things we're ever called upon to do, and we have to do it when we're least equipped to handle the challenge. If only we could grow up before we have to grow up. That would make everything a lot easier.

Here's how it happens instead.

One day you get dropped off at a bus stop and you're told to figure out the way home by yourself. But first you've got to figure out what home is. You may have had some instructions drilled into you, but you're still on your own. Some young people, like Nate, get more lost than others. I was one of those who got *really* lost and wandered from bus stop to bus stop for about 15 years. I spent the first few years clutching the wrong city map before I realized it. After getting that straightened out, I held the map upside down for the longest time and made no progress at all.

Now I look back and wonder why it had to be so difficult. I knew where home was all along. So did Saint Augustine, and this is how he described it: "You have made us for yourself, O Lord, and our heart is restless until it rests in you."

I looked at Nate and saw myself—an earnest young man with a lot of questions, holding the wrong city map in his hands and trying desperately to get home. We had a few minutes before the next class, so I shared my story with him. "I'm not going to try to convert you," I said, which surprised him. He laughed nervously. "But I want you to know it's possible to come out on the other side believing."

From that point on I took a special interest in Nate. I gave him a book to read and made a point of asking how he was doing. I told him my office door was always open to him. Nate wasn't an evangelistic project to me, and I didn't see him as a potential jewel in my heavenly crown. He was a young man lost in a great big city. He was a young version of me.

About halfway through the semester Nate stopped coming to class, and I don't know what happened to him. But I hope he makes his way back home. I hope he tells me someday that heaven opened up again and that his story ended well, just the way it's supposed to.

I think of what Jesus told Nathanael—call him Nate, if you will—about what lay in store for the one who follows him in faith: "'I tell you the truth, you shall see heaven open, and the angels of God ascending and descending on the Son of Man'" (John 1:51).

A Locked Room Mystery

When we struggle with our faith, it's good to remember how frequently, how intensely, and how stupidly the disciples doubted. This is one of those quirky but powerful pieces of evidence that points to the authenticity of the Gospels. There's no attempt to sanitize their biographies or make them super-spiritual. The Gospels don't paint halos around their heads.

The disciples were flesh-and-blood men who struggled to believe even when the Evidence, the risen Lord, was standing right before them.

The disciples aren't stained-glass saints but flesh-and-blood men who struggled to believe even when the Evidence, the risen Lord, was standing right before them.

Thomas is the one we usually think of. He's the most famous doubter in the Bible—so famous that we've nicknamed him *Doubting* Thomas. But there's so much more to Thomas than that. Ancient church tradition says he carried the gospel all the way to India, and there are good reasons to believe the story may be true. That's pretty good work for a skeptic.

Even in the Gospels we catch glimpses of how remarkable he was, this intellectual who approached the world on the basis of what was possible and probable. His mind kept getting in the way, but his heart was wholly committed to Christ. After Lazarus died, Jesus began to move toward Bethany where he would face certain danger from his enemies. The disciples must have hesitated. Fear must have paralyzed them. I'm reading between the lines, but it's a plausible reconstruction given what Thomas said next. "'Let us also go, that we may die with him'" (John 11:16). He displayed courage, loyalty, and affection—and he rallied the disciples under his leadership. There's no doubt about it, Thomas deserves better from us.

The famous scene, the doubting scene, occurs in a locked room. Thomas hadn't been with Peter and John when they ran to the garden that Sunday morning. He was a rational man, and he was trying to get his bearings in a landscape that had suddenly shifted. Thomas thought he knew the way home. He thought he had the map. It was Thomas, after all, who asked, "Lord, we don't know where you are going, so how can we know the way?" That question prompted the great reply: "'I am the way and the truth and the life. No one comes to the Father except through me'" (John 14:5-6).

That's the map Thomas was holding in his hands the day Jesus died. Days later Thomas was still trying to figure things out: "A week later his disciples were in the house again, and Thomas was with them. Though the doors were locked, Jesus came and stood among them and said, 'Peace be with you!'" (John 20:26).

So why did Jesus appear to Thomas in a locked room? I'm sure Thomas didn't read murder mysteries; but if he had, he would have appreciated the irony. A locked room was the ultimate setup for Agatha Christie. A murder victim is found in a room that's locked from the inside. *Where did the killer go?* A whole mystery subgenre has been built around this premise. A locked-room mystery is an intellectual puzzle that focuses the powers of rational thought. Only observation, reason, and logic can penetrate the seemingly impossible set of circumstances. If the mystery is to be solved at all, it will be through sheer brainpower. Chance plays no part.

Jesus was making a point, I'm sure. He appeared to Mary in the garden. He appeared to two disciples on a road outside Jerusalem. He appeared to scores of believers throughout Galilee. But for Thomas—he had to appear inside a locked room.

Jesus might have said, "Go ahead, Thomas. Try to figure the puzzle out." But incredibly, and lovingly, he subjected himself to the analysis: "Then he said to Thomas, 'Put your finger here; see my hands. Reach out your hand and put it into my side. Stop doubting and believe'" (John 20:27). John doesn't tell us if Thomas followed through. All he tells us is that Thomas responded the only way he could—with an exclamation of faith: "'My Lord, and my God!'" (v. 28).

Trust and Obey

The great seventeenth-century Italian painter Caravaggio sensed the dramatic intensity of this moment. He must have seen himself in Thomas—a man who struggled to believe, a man whose life was grounded in the material world. Caravaggio was the most brilliant and controversial artist of his age. He was also a drunkard and a rabble-rouser—a man who fled for his life after killing a man in a tavern brawl. But when he turned his brush to the great scenes of the Bible, nobody has ever matched his genius. Nobody has come close to the earthiness and candor of his artistic vision.

Through Caravaggio's eyes, we see Thomas leaning toward Jesus. His brow is furrowed and his eyes are wide open. Two other disciples lean over his shoulder with looks of astonishment. Caravaggio senses the truth behind the story. *These other disciples had been doubting too.* You can see it in their faces.

With one hand Jesus pulls aside his garment to reveal the wound. With his other hand, Jesus grips the wrist of the doubting disciple and guides his hand toward his side, into the cavity of the wound, a fold of flesh where the Roman soldier had thrust a spear. The painting bristles with tension. Jesus is forcing the issue, bringing Thomas's finger, the very instrument of his sense and reason, into contact with the scarred flesh.

We always single Thomas out. *He's* the doubting disciple, we say, when in reality he was the *honest* one. For 40 days Jesus appeared to the disciples. He taught them. He ate with them. It took 40 days of evidence because it wasn't easy for them to believe. They may have been ordinary men, not research scientists with PhDs after their names, but they *knew* that dead bodies don't live again.

Right before he commissioned them to "go and make disciples of all nations" (Matthew 28:19), Jesus appeared to the 11 disciples at one time. He sent them to Galilee and told them to go to a certain mountain. Perhaps this was the place where he had delivered the Sermon on the Mount. Perhaps it was one of the desolate places where Jesus often withdrew from the crowds to be alone with his Father. We don't know where this mountain was, but the disciples obeyed, and they were waiting for him.

Matthew tells us what happened when Jesus arrived. "When they saw him, they worshiped him; *but some doubted*" (Matthew 28:17, emphasis added). Some doubted! They had believed enough to follow his instructions; but when Jesus showed up on time, they must have thought he was a ghost.

It wasn't just Thomas who doubted. It's all of us.

You see, it wasn't just Thomas who doubted. It's all of us. We know too much about the world to believe easily. And we know too much not to believe. And so Jesus directs us to the mountain. He appears to us again. And we worship him again—even when we sometimes doubt.

By the time 40 days were up, the disciples were ready to go into all the world and tell us what they had seen. They stood with Jesus one last time and witnessed one more miracle. The heavens opened.

The heavens opened—and Jesus went home.

I wonder what Thomas was thinking as he watched Jesus disappear. Perhaps he remembered what the Lord said shortly before going to the cross. Jesus wanted his disciples to trust and obey even when nothing made sense. "'Do not let your hearts be troubled,'" Jesus said. "'Trust in God; trust also in me'" (John 14:1). He knew their hearts would be shaken with fear.

Our doubts often come down to a failure of trust, not of belief. Trust is all about commitment. The King James Version of this passage is perhaps so familiar to us ("Ye believe in God, believe also in me") that we can fail to see this distinction. It's commitment that Jesus is speaking about—a deep, resolute decision of the heart, not some intellectual affirmation. Trust is what Thomas had already demonstrated. Thomas, after all, had been willing to die for Jesus (John 11:16).

Our doubts often come down to a failure of trust, not of belief.

Jesus told the disciples to trust him, to commit themselves to him without reservation, because he was about to make a startling claim.

> "In my Father's house are many rooms; if it were not so, I would have told you. I am going there to prepare a place for you. And if I go and prepare a place for you, I will come back and take you to be with me that you also may be where I am. You know the way to the place where I am going" (John 14:2-4).

That's when Thomas jumped in with his logical question, "'Lord, we don't know where you are going, so how can we know the way?'" (v. 5). Jesus presented himself as the answer: "'I am the way and the truth and the life'" (v. 6). We need to correctly label our doubts as failures to commit ourselves not to some idea, not to a set of propositions or a process of logical argumentation, but to a person, to Jesus Christ.

I wonder if this transcript was playing in Thomas's head as he watched the Lord disappear into the clouds. *I will come back and take you to be with me that you also may be where I am.* Thomas stood at the threshold of all that God intended for him. The heavens opened, and he entered in by faith to the promises of God. He was ready now to catch the next ship to India.

This is how I would challenge the intellectual doubter like Nate. Maybe for you the question is not "How can I believe?" but rather "How can I trust?" You've seen and experienced the goodness of God. Now go and trust him—commit yourself to him. Trust that God will open the heavens so you can enjoy all he's preparing for you, every good thing that has your name on it.

But in order to trust him with our hearts, we need to understand what to do with our heads. This doesn't mean denying reason and retreating into mysticism and irrationality. God created us to think as well as feel, and we must love him with "all our minds" (Matthew 22:37). We need to recognize, however, that reason is just part of the package that God created. Reason can take us only so far toward God. That's why I have four questions for Nate—and for anyone who struggles with intellectual doubt.

- What's so special about reason?
- Does faith always have to be a house of cards?
- Do you take seriously the limits of human knowledge?
- When is reason just an excuse for living a self-oriented life?

Like a Stradivarius

Faith is like a Stradivarius, those legendary instruments the Stradivari family fashioned by hand in the early eighteenth century. Antonio Stradivari died in 1737 after having crafted some 1100 violins, violas, cellos, guitars, along with a harp or two—nearly 700 of which survive today. They are the most highly prized musical instruments ever made, fetching as much as two to three million dollars at auction.

So what's the big deal with a Stradivarius? Quite simply, it can't be duplicated. Every instrument of science can be brought to bear on the instruments of Stradivarius and yet fail to quantify what makes it a *Stradivarius*. Nobody can reduce to a formula the unique musical tone of these instruments, and that should remind us that there are reservoirs of knowledge that lie deeper than reason's ability to measure. Hungarian scientist and philosopher Michael Polanyi evoked the famous violins as an example of the limitations of rational knowledge.

> *There are areas of knowledge that don't yield themselves to the methods of science.*

It is pathetic to watch the endless efforts—equipped with microscopy and chemistry, with mathematics and electronics—to reproduce a single violin of the kind the half-literate Stradivarius turned out as a matter of routine more than 200 years ago.

"We always know more than we can tell" is the well-known summary of Polanyi's theory of knowledge. There are areas of knowledge that don't yield themselves to the methods of science. There is truth that can't be reduced to quantitative analysis. We could easily list many examples, as Polanyi does, of knowledge that is real but intangible. The wine taster, for example, draws upon a body of experience that can't be transcribed into a textbook. This "more than we can tell" quality is not subject to rational methodologies. This knowledge is intuitive, or "tacit" (as Polanyi termed it); but it's no less real and no less true.

None of this is surprising to the Christian. We believe in a God who is transcendent of human knowledge. The Christian believes that ultimate reality is not measurable. When Job was suffering his great personal loss and agonizing over the silence of God, his friends offered him many theories—some good and some bad—about the way the world works. Zophar took a crack at the great cosmic mystery by describing God as boundless. He used the dimensions that give us volume to describe a God who has no limit.

> "Can you fathom the mysteries of God?
> Can you probe the limits of the Almighty?

They are higher than the heavens—what can you do?
They are deeper than the depths of the grave—
    what can you know?
Their measure is longer than the earth
    and wider than the sea."

(Job 11:7-9)

Height and depth, length and width. Can we put God in a box, even if it's a really big one?

The ancient Greeks knew all about measurements and divine proportions. Their temples were based upon the so-called Golden Rectangle—a mathematical equation that recurs mysteriously throughout nature. But standing in Athens, with the greatest of these temples, the Parthenon, as his backdrop, Paul rejected the idea that God can be confined to any space of human imagining: "The God who made the world and everything in it is the Lord of heaven and earth and does not live in temples built by hands" (Acts 17:24).

When writing to the church at Ephesus, Paul seemed to pick up on Zophar's description of the limitlessness of God. In so doing, he laid out the Christian answer to the problem of God's transcendence. Christ completely fills out the infinite dimensions of God.

So that Christ may dwell in your hearts through faith. And I pray that you, being rooted and established in love, may have power, together with all the saints, to grasp how *wide and long and high and deep* is the love of Christ (Ephesians 3:17-18, emphasis added).

The great mystery here is that we are *in Christ* and Christ is *in us*. This is how the limitless and transcendent God can be known. Christ is the violin maker, and he is shaping us into a Stradivarius. This kind of knowledge lies beyond human reason.

So what's so special about reason? Why do we elevate the rational methods of science, logic, and mathematics above other ways of knowing? Every intellectual doubter, and every smug skeptic, should wrestle with these questions and not merely assume that reason and science form the bedrock beneath every statement that is true.

Ever since the eighteenth-century Enlightenment, the so-called Age of Reason, the Western world has invested itself heavily in the idea that rational inquiry discovers, determines, and defines what is truth. The rational mind would point to spaceships and airplanes as though the machines we make are eloquent refutations of religion. It was the science of physics, after all, and not the doctrine of the Trinity that put a man on the moon. That would seem to settle the matter in reason's favor.

But that's where the Stradivarius becomes an inconvenient intrusion. Not every type of knowledge, not every form of experience, can be pressed into an equation. The claim of Scripture is that Christ is the repository of wisdom (Colossians 2:3). The doubter needs to know that this is as good a claim as any.

House of Cards

There were many good things about the little fundamentalist church I grew up in. A clear understanding of faith, unfortunately, was not one of them. The people were loving and sincere. The pastor earnestly believed and faithfully taught the Bible. But faith and doubt were never clearly explained to the seven-year-old who stood up one Sunday in front of the congregation and sang "Rescue the Perishing."

But who would rescue the doubting? When I started to doubt, who would rescue me?

Oh, I understood as a child that one must have "personal faith in Jesus Christ" in order to be saved. But along with that came a long list of interlocking propositions and cultural values. If any of these were challenged and rejected, the entire system would be threatened. All around me were slippery slopes, and the key to never falling was to hold on tight to every single proposition.

But the metaphor isn't as relevant to me anymore. Where the fundamentalists once saw a slippery slope, I now see a house of cards.

I do look back with great appreciation to the fundamentalist legacy of the early twentieth century. These were godly men—R.A. Torrey, G. Campbell Morgan, and others—who took seriously the historic claims of Christianity. But one of the unfortunate by-products of fundamentalism has been the "house of cards" approach to faith. Pull one card out and the whole structure—so delicately, intricately, and impressively balanced—utterly collapses. Christianity was presented to me as a package deal, in which faith in X is equated with faith in Y and Z.

X (the Greek letter *chi*, pronounced "kē" or "kī") is the ancient Christian symbol for Christ—*Christos*, or *Xristos*, in the Greek. The great crux of our faith, literally, is an X, a cross—"Christ crucified" as Paul summarizes it in 1 Corinthians 2:2. Faith in X is what matters. Y and Z might be important, and we may have convictions about defending them; but Y and Z are not the same as X.

In its zeal to defend biblical truth, fundamentalism didn't think clearly about what happens when we tether Christ to anything but the cross.

Fundamentalism set out to defend the faith, but for many it became instead a graveyard for faith. Here's where the hard questions come—the ones that divide Christians into camps. Do you need to be a young-earth creationist to be a Christian? Do you have to insist on a certain kind of rigid biblical literalism?

Now I happen to think there are good reasons to believe the earth is relatively young, even if creation didn't occur at precisely 9:00 a.m. on October 3, 4004 BC as a seventeenth-century theologian claimed. Some Christians, however, earnestly defend the *necessity* of a particular interpretation of the age of the earth. A house of cards is carefully erected. A whole progression of arguments is leveraged. The age of the earth is tightly connected in a logical but extrabiblical way to the atoning work of Christ. Rejecting young-earth creationism thus becomes equivalent to rejecting Christ.

Does faith have to be a house of cards? No—and it shouldn't be. Christ is the only dividing line. I don't want to leverage every doctrine against Jesus Christ. Paul draws his line in the sand very clearly: "That if you confess with your mouth, 'Jesus is Lord,' and believe in your heart that God raised him from the dead, you will be saved" (Romans 10:9).

> *Paul understood that faith in Christ—not the age of the earth or the Mosaic authorship of the Pentateuch—is the dividing line between life with God and life without him.*

Paul wasn't lax in defending sound doctrine. He didn't have a devil-may-care attitude toward false teachings and practices in the church. But he did understand that faith in Christ—not the age of the earth or the Mosaic authorship of the Pentateuch—is the dividing line between life with God and life without him.

Jesus asked the disciples, "Who do you say I am?" (Matthew 16:15). He didn't ask them what their view of creation was, as important as this is. The dividing line has always been Christ. Nothing more and nothing less. It's always a tragedy when people reject Christ over a house of cards that men have constructed.

A Little Extra Baggage

It's a virtue to travel lightly. But we don't always have the choice. I've taken several mission trips to India, and whenever I go, I try to minimize my baggage. Navigating through the Delhi airport, I've found, is much easier when I travel light. The problem I run into, however, is that I'm going to be visiting missionary friends in India who need things. And they have family back home who want to send things overseas—using Mike's Overnight Delivery Service, nonstop from Newark to Delhi. There's always one more bag ("Don't worry, it's small"), always one more bundle—and then my transformation from missionary to pack mule is complete. I want to travel like Indiana Jones, but I end up like Ma Joad in *The Grapes of Wrath,* sitting atop her Model T and tooling her way toward California with all her earthly possessions. Once I'm committed to the trip, however, I'm committed to the extra baggage.

Faith is like that—but so is doubt.

With every presupposition comes baggage. If you believe in a personal, all-powerful God who is good, then you've acquired, as part of the package deal, a set of questions about evil and human suffering. But the atheist has his own set of questions too. What is the source and nature of goodness in the world? If we're just bundles of chemistry, then why do we create art and poetry, believe there is purpose in life, and worship a God we cannot see? If we're only material beings, then wouldn't it be more natural for these behaviors to be peculiarities and anomalies? Instead, they are the factory setting of the human soul.

> *It's fair to demand that the believer believe his beliefs; but it's also fair to demand that the doubter doubt his doubts.*

The atheist, of course, has answers for these questions, just as the theist has answers for the problem of evil and suffering. But where the theist has to explain only the origin of evil, the atheist has to explain (or explain away) the origin of both evil and good. Go ahead and pick which task you think is more difficult. In the end, neither side can neutralize the other through argumentation. It's fair to demand that the believer believe his beliefs; but it's also fair to demand that the doubter doubt his doubts. Skeptics can be hypocrites as surely as Christians can.

This leads to my third question for Nate: *Do you take seriously the limits of human knowledge?* Questions about evil and suffering demand this of religion—demand, that is, that we concede the limits of faith. But the claims of reason also invite a whole series of questions about the world. The skeptic can choose to dismiss these questions as enigmas that science will someday unravel. Indeed, the chemical consistency of faith may someday be demonstrated. The specific neural reaction that we call *joy* or *wonder* or *nostalgia* may someday be decoded and transcribed as a mathematical equation.

But I doubt that will ever happen—and I'm not alone in that hunch. Many scientists, many with no faith in a personal God, recognize that our knowledge has real thresholds. Science will succeed in removing all that is ineffable right around the time it figures out how to duplicate a Stradivarius. I'm inclined to think that the mystery of life, the mystery of consciousness, and the mystery of the cosmos are somewhat more complex than the task of constructing a single violin. Once we've made that concession, then we've conceded the possibility that some barriers cannot be crossed.

Guess what? There's enough elbow room in that one concession for a universe of faith.

Dirty Rivers

In the end, we exercise our will to believe or not believe. Whatever side we end up on, we'll still have questions. And so we have to choose how we're going to live—either with God or without him. That's what my final question is all about: *When is reason just an excuse for living a self-oriented life?*

Faith is a choice. The story of Naaman the leper (2 Kings 5:1-19) shows us that reason can cut two ways. Reason can lead us to reject the more peculiar claims of revelation, or reason can lead us, in our desperation, to embrace what we don't understand.

Naaman was a powerful, self-confident man, a general in Syria who was afflicted with leprosy. When the story opens, we see a man who starts off with faith. He believed a most unlikely witness—a little Jewish girl who served in his house. The servant girl told Naaman that Elisha the prophet could heal him. Faith often has embarrassing beginnings like this. Faith requires the proud man to stoop down and listen to a child. Faith requires the powerful man to admit his weakness. Faith requires the leprous man to look in the mirror and describe accurately what he sees.

> *The pursuit of self over God often disguises itself in the respectable clothing of rational thought.*

Naaman took the next step and acted on what he believed. He searched out the prophet for himself: "So Naaman went with his horses and chariots and stopped at the door of Elisha's house" (2 Kings 5:9). In the language of the Bible, horses and chariots always speak of pride. "Some trust in chariots and some in horses," David wrote, "but we trust in the name of the Lord our God" (Psalm 20:7). This is our first clue that Naaman had not yet come to the end of himself. He was not yet desperate enough for God.

When Naaman arrived at Elisha's doorstep, the prophet wouldn't even come out to see him. Instead, Elisha sent his assistant out with God's instructions: "Go, wash yourself seven times in the Jordan." Naaman took one look at the Jordan—a muddy, unremarkable river—and his doubts started settling in. He must have felt foolish for believing the little girl in the first place. His pride, his sense of dignity, began crowding out faith. Theologians have a fancy way of describing what Naaman felt. It's called "the scandal of particularity." Why *this* river? Why not some *other* river, like the one back home in Syria?

God's call to faith is not meant to be easy. It may require us to step into a dirty river and sacrifice our dignity. But it always requires us to confront the greatest scandal of all, Christ himself. Christ is the stumbling block, or *scandalon* in the Greek. He's an offense to our rational faculty (1 Corinthians 1:23). He doesn't make sense to us. In coming to Christ, we must walk away from self-reliance, self-interest, self-composure, self-sufficiency, self-image. And that's where reason often applies the brakes to faith. The pursuit of *self* over God often disguises itself in the respectable clothing of rational thought.

But reason can cut two ways. In the end, Naaman came back to faith when his servants reasoned with him. The arguments they made were compelling. *We've come a long way to turn back empty-handed. It's not really that big a deal—just do what the old man said. What do you have to lose?* Naaman's servants presented him with an early version of Pascal's Wager. The seventeenth-century French philosopher Pascal posed these questions: "What do you have to lose if you embrace God and you're wrong? Now, what do you have to lose if you reject God—and you're wrong?" That's the wager, and it's a reasonable way to consider the stakes. Naaman stepped into the water, and "his flesh was restored and became clean like that of a young boy" (2 Kings 5:14).

The Windows Open

A couple of chapters after the story of Naaman, we read about some more lepers who were struggling with faith and doubt. The city of Samaria was besieged by the Aramean army, and the people were dying of starvation. The situation had become so dire that people were even resorting to cannibalism (2 Kings 6:24-29).

Elisha prophesied that the famine would be over in a single day and that food would be plentiful once more in the marketplace (2 Kings 7:1). The prophesy was so outrageous, so out of touch with reality, that one of the king's officers openly mocked the prophet's words. "'If the LORD himself should make windows in heaven,'" he said, "'could this thing be?'" (v. 2 ESV). What the prophet said didn't make any sense. It didn't seem *rational*—and so reason became the excuse for this man's unbelief.

Meanwhile, four lepers sat outside the wall as outcasts from the city. They sized up the situation and began to reason among themselves. "'Why stay here until we die?'" they asked each other. They reasoned that if they entered the city, they'd die of famine. If they stayed outside the wall, they'd also die of famine. "'So let's go over to the camp of the Arameans and surrender. If they spare us, we live; if they kill us, then we die'" (vv. 3-4). Reason became the instrument of faith for these desperate men. When faced with a wager for which the stakes were life and death, they committed themselves to a reasonable choice.

They "rose up in the twilight" (v. 5 KJV) and walked straight toward the enemy. God saw their desperation and delivered them. As this pathetic troop of lepers advanced toward the Aramean camp, God miraculously confounded the enemy. The Arameans heard "the sound of chariots and horses and a great army" approaching (v. 6). They fled from their camp, abandoning everything they had—food, clothing, silver, and gold.

God saw faith and he opened the windows of heaven. The lepers, and the city of Samaria, were spared. The famine was over. And the officer who mocked God was trampled to death in the city gate as the people rushed out to plunder the camp.

God's answers to our doubts are not always this dramatic. But when we "rise up in the twilight" as these lepers did, we'll find that God's hand has been resting on the window latch all along.

Summing-Up: Sometimes the heavens seem shut to us. We ask questions that have no answers. Those who have intellectual doubts, as the apostle Thomas did, need to know there are good reasons for believing in God. There are limits to human reason. Science cannot explain everything. Faith is a reasonable response to questions that are bigger than we are.

For Further Reflection

1. The story of Naaman shows that reason can drive us toward faith and away from faith. What role does reason play in the story of the Prodigal Son (Luke 15:11-24)?

2. Do you have a "house of cards" view of faith? If so, what are the doctrines or beliefs that have been leveraged against your faith in Christ?

3. What things do you *know* that can't be rationally explained or expressed?

4. If Caravaggio were to paint you as Doubting Thomas, what details should he emphasize? How should he portray your facial expression or body language?

CHAPTER 7

A Foot in Both Worlds

Key Idea: **When we see God's hand in the world around us, we're already halfway to faith.**

MY DOG, SCRUFFY, DOESN'T BELIEVE IN ANYTHING, as best I can determine. He's a wonderful dog, a faithful companion, a bit obsessive about shoes at times, and quite loud when other dogs are strutting down the street with their owners in tow.

But his spiritual life is utterly lacking. He stays home when we go to church—which is probably good since he's a rat terrier, and rat terriers have great difficulty sitting still for long. Each morning when we read our family devotions, Scruffy is casing the breakfast table, looking for handouts, scouting possible laps to invade. Altogether, he seems completely uninterested in the things of God.

But, of course, I don't worry about it. That's how God made him. There's not one ounce of faith in his 13 pounds of energy.

In a simple but subtle way, Jesus pointed this out—not about Scruffy but about the Galilean countryside. "Think about the birds of the air," he said as a lead-in to some rather simple observations about nature (Matthew 6:26-30). *Birds don't fret about their food. They don't worry about their next meal. And yet God in heaven feeds them.* "Consider the lily." *The flowers of the field don't toil or weave, and yet they're clothed more lavishly than Solomon.*

We're not likely to find the "field notes" of Jesus written up in a *Scientific*

American article. Looked at one way, his observations can strike us as completely unremarkable. This is one of the reasons why it's easy to misunderstand Jesus and fail to grasp the depth of what he said. He seems to be making elementary, even obvious, statements about lilies and birds.

But is this so?

Halfway to Faith

The best way to hear Jesus teach is to close our eyes until we can feel the Galilean sun on our cheeks and the warm breeze as it blows off the lake. We should be able to hear the birds and inhale the sweet fragrance of blossoms on the wind. Jesus never shied away from the physical world. He never denied or rejected that we are material beings. This fact was the starting point for his teaching about the Kingdom of Heaven or the Kingdom of God. When our feet are planted firmly in the world of God's creation, then we're already halfway to faith.

The child understands this, which is why Jesus turned to children so often as an example. When it rains, the child wants to get wet and taste the rain on his tongue. Wherever there's a puddle, there's a child jumping in for the sheer pleasure of the splash. The littlest among us know that mud exists only so we can press our wiggling toes into the ooze. On warm summer evenings, children sense that there's one very important thing left to do before bedtime—chase fireflies and collect them in a Mason jar.

> *Doubt is a dullness of the senses.*

I don't want to concede the world to anybody. Not to the Buddhist poet writing haiku in seventeenth-century Japan. Not to the environmentalist in twenty-first century America or the Romantic poet in nineteenth-century England. Nature isn't my god, but I want to have a robust, bodily faith like that of a child. I want to sink my toes into the muddy wonders of God's creation.

Doubt is a dullness of the senses. Jesus wants us to know that faith starts by being grounded in the world. Jesus isn't saying, "Look up and have faith." He's saying, "*Look around you and have faith.* See what God is already doing— and have faith." Our faith, Jesus says, is a reasonable response to how God does things in the world. He's fully engaged in ways we don't always see. Jesus wants his disciples to open their eyes to this. We may not see the hand of God clothing the lily or feeding the bird—but that's the work of God nonetheless. My failure to see God's hand in the world is one of the most basic reasons why I doubt.

Yes, we have a foot in both worlds. We're part of creation. Our physical lives are bound up in "seedtime and harvest" (Genesis 8:22). Our conscious experience is woven into the fabric of this world.

But who we are ultimately transcends the rhythms and routines of our days. We're more than just material beings, though faith begins with a foot in *this* world. Wherever you're standing right now, no matter what your doubts may be, you're already halfway to faith. This is what Jesus is saying in part. Faith requires us to plant one foot in the world, pivot, and then step toward God.

The Great Divide

Easier said than done, right? The gulf between body and spirit seems to grow wider as we leave childhood behind. So let's return to the simple formula:

We doubt because we're made from the dust of the earth.
We believe because God breathed into us the breath of life.

We are of two worlds—heaven and earth. This is the basic paradox of the human condition. Our dual nature holds the key to why we doubt and why we have an instinct to believe. To deny either doubt or faith is to deny an essential part of who we are.

The conviction that we are "body and spirit" is not some exotic view held by a few people once in a while throughout history. It's the default view; it's the commonsense view, which simply means the view *held in common.* Most people living at most times have taken it for granted that there is an "I" somewhere at the center of my existence. This "I," and all it represents when I use the first person pronoun, is not the same thing as my physical body.

I have a body, and my body is made up of physical properties that can be described in chemical and biological terms. But I'm speaking of something deeper than my skin when I say "I." Think about it. The pronoun makes sense only if there's something *there*, something that feels and believes and knows and loves and worships.

It's fashionable for materialists today to deny there's any "I" behind these expressions. The self, they say, is an elaborate illusion. We're nothing more than a highly evolved biological machine that has found convenient ways to deceive itself. This view has gained traction in the Western world, but it's very much an anomaly. It's the rare exception in human culture. It might be the sophisticated view of the intellectual elite, but it's utter foolishness.

The ancient Greek philosophers understood this dichotomy over 2000 years ago. Plato tells us, through the voice of Socrates, about the so-called "first philosopher." Thales (pronounced THAY-leez) was walking along observing the heavens with such deep philosophical concentration that he didn't see the well in front of him. He fell in. Along came a servant girl who peered down at him in the well and made a joke about how he was so busy looking up that he didn't watch his own feet. Plato then gives us the point of the whole matter. What happened to Thales, he says, is typical of philosophers.

> *The secular intellectual may deny that anything transcends the here and now, but he keeps finding, much to his surprise, that heaven has a low ceiling.*

And it's also true of secular intellectuals today, though we'd have to reverse the terms. Focused intently on the *ground*—the grounding of our material existence—the secular intellectual keeps hitting his head. He may deny that anything transcends the here and now, but he keeps finding, much to his surprise, that heaven has a low ceiling.

Nevertheless, the secularist remains committed to defining human life in purely material terms. Public policy experts at the United Nations, for example, have developed statistical indexes to rank nations based on their standard of living, quality of life, or even happiness and satisfaction. The Human Development Index (HDI) scores and ranks nations according to life expectancy, literacy, and per capita Gross Domestic Product (GDP), which is essentially buying power as translated into a standard of living. According to these materialistic metrics, most of the highly ranked nations are found in western Europe.

Those nations with the highest HDI ranking tend to be the most thoroughly secularized places in the world—and this would seem to vindicate the materialist view of life. But these nations are slowly imploding from a catastrophic demographic imbalance. Dropping birth rates cannot sustain the fiscal demands of a social-welfare bureaucracy, and the promise of a secular "heaven on earth" is turning out to be an illusion. Somebody has to pay the bills if you're going to live in heaven. The wisdom of this world is like Thales, only this time it's public-policy experts who are staring at the ground while ignoring heaven altogether. There is no spiritual quotient at all in the HDI, so it fails to give us the whole picture.

If people were countries, Jesus would have ranked pretty low on the Human Development Index—I'm guessing somewhere around Zimbabwe. His life expectancy was short. He didn't have a home or a steady job. "'Foxes have holes,'" Jesus said, "'and birds of the air have nests, but the Son of Man has no place to lay his head'" (Matthew 8:20). Jesus loved a good meal as much as anyone (Matthew 11:19), but his standard of living wasn't set by the world. "'My food,'" Jesus said, "'is to do the will of him who sent me and to finish his work'" (John 4:34).

> *John wants us to know that doubting is necessary to a faith that's truly grounded.*

Jesus knew that we were created for more than the HDI can possibly gauge. So he came to those who were spiritually blind, men and women deadened by the routines of life. He called them to look beyond the narrow confines of flesh and blood to the greater purpose God has for us. And then he called them to step toward that purpose by faith. This grand invitation to step beyond the great divide into the Kingdom of Heaven is seen most clearly in the Gospel of John.

John's Optics

John tells us plainly what he's up to in the fourth Gospel—the one that breaks the mold. Matthew, Mark, and Luke follow the same basic plan. Scholars call them the "synoptic Gospels"—literally, "Gospels that see together." But John's optics are a little different. John looks at Jesus from the perspective of faith. It's as though John is standing on one side of the great divide and encouraging us to step across as well. "These [things] are written," he tells us, "that you may believe" (John 20:31).

So that's it—that's the plan. John is writing a faith manual. He wants us to know what faith is. He also wants us to know that doubting is necessary to a faith that's truly grounded. John wants us to know how we believe, why we believe, and who we should believe in. And he wants us to know that faith, reason, and experience all work together.

All through the Gospel of John we see encounters between Jesus and ordinary men and women. These encounters give us a template of faith. They show us how disorienting it is when Jesus calls us out from the world of sense and experience. We live in a world that is solid and real to us; it's a world of routines and predictable causes and effects. Jesus tells us there's much more than this—much more that God has designed us for. We struggle to wrap our minds around it. Jesus speaks, and we stumble over his words. We see this over and over throughout the Gospel of John, beginning with the story of Nicodemus.

> Now there was a man of the Pharisees named Nicodemus, a member of the Jewish ruling council. He came to Jesus at night and said, "Rabbi, we know you are a teacher who has come from God. For no one could perform the miraculous signs you are doing if God were not with him" (John 3:1-2).

Jesus gets right to the point. He makes no attempt to ease Nicodemus into the deeper truths of God; rather, Jesus confronts him immediately with the most improbable claim of all.

> In reply Jesus declared, "I tell you the truth, no one can see the kingdom of God unless he is born again" (v. 3).

What Jesus says makes no sense to him. Nicodemus is at a critical point—the decisive point between faith and unbelief. That's the middle ground, the halfway point called "doubt." But he isn't ready to give up yet. He doesn't turn away in contempt. He brings his questions back to Jesus.

> "How can a man be born when he is old?" Nicodemus asked. "Surely he cannot enter a second time into his mother's womb to be born!" (v. 4)

It's a reasonable question—one rooted in his rational understanding of the world. Grown men do not enter a second time into their mother's wombs to be born. Jesus responds by saying that "'no one can enter the kingdom of

God unless he is born of water and the Spirit'" (v. 5). There's some disagreement about what Jesus meant. It may be that he was referring to the prophecy of the New Covenant that Ezekiel delivered when Israel was in captivity (Ezekiel 36:25-27). It's also reasonable to identify water with physical birth and the Spirit with spiritual birth. Jesus may be saying we need two births, physical and spiritual, to see the Kingdom of God.

This passage is usually taught with the emphasis placed almost exclusively on the spiritual birth—the "being born again" part of the equation. But Jesus says we need two births. What this means is that we can't see God's kingdom without a physical birth too. God designed us to be both physical and spiritual, which means we need "a foot in both worlds" in order to enter God's kingdom. The angels are spiritual beings too, but they don't have bodies as we do. Though they dwell in the presence of God, they cannot "see the kingdom of God" in the same sense that we can. Jesus is speaking of entering into voluntary submission to God's sovereign reign, which is a privilege reserved for those made in God's image. We who are made of dust can choose to follow God in the earthly sphere that he created, and in so doing, enter into his kingdom. Our physical bodies and the material world were always a part of God's plan.

Nicodemus sets the pattern for every encounter that follows in the Gospel of John. The questions are unrelenting. It all starts when someone comes to Jesus—or Jesus comes to them, as is the case in John 4 with the Samaritan woman.

Jesus went out of his way to go through Samaria, to stop by a well, and to meet a woman there. He was thirsty, and so he asked for a drink. As the conversation unfolded, Jesus drew this ordinary woman to faith. He challenged her to start with what she already knew about the world. A deep drink of water is really satisfying when you're thirsty. This is what she knew, and that's why she was already halfway to faith. Jesus invited her to go further, however, and look beyond the physical water to the great spiritual truth that gives it meaning. Water is a wonderfully satisfying thing on a hot and dusty day, but it's only a small hint of what lies beyond.

The moment of faith always comes when we first catch a glimpse beyond the seemingly solid wall of the material world.

Jesus began to tell her about living water, but she struggled with the meaning. She pressed his words into the only categories she knew. *Water comes from a well that's dug into the ground. It's lifted up in a bucket and then poured into pitchers.* "'Sir, you have nothing to draw with,'" she said, "'and the well is deep. Where can you get this living water?'" (John 4:11). Her doubts were reasonable and her questions were based in the world of experience. She didn't understand, but she didn't turn away from Jesus either. She reached out, like Nicodemus, to what she couldn't see.

Over and over the pattern repeats itself. Jesus speaks of ordinary things, but he's always referring to something extraordinary. Men and women hear his words, but they stumble over the literal, material forms. "'I have spoken to you of earthly things,'" Jesus said, "'and you do not believe; how then will you believe if I speak of heavenly things?'" (John 3:12). The moment of faith always comes when we first catch a glimpse beyond the seemingly solid wall of the material world. This is when we understand that the world of forms, the world of experience, the world of sensation and feeling, even the world of rationality and logic, makes sense only because something much greater lies behind it.

Wonderful Bread

I don't remember a whole lot about my elementary school days. But a few things stick out in my memory—a few moments, a few field trips, like the one my class took to the Wonder Bread bakery. Wonder Bread is an American classic that goes back to 1925—sliced, bleached, American white bread, pumped full of vitamins and preservatives.

In the great desert of my childhood memory, why do I remember this field trip? Maybe it was the yeasty smell. Maybe it was the huge vats of flour and the busy conveyor belts. Maybe it was the miniature loaf of Wonder Bread given to every student at the end of the tour.

There was something wonderful, I suppose, about perfectly formed loaves of bread dropping off a conveyor belt, ready to be packaged in colorful bags and shipped off to the grocery store. But there's something far more wonderful that we read in the Gospel of John.

The feeding of the 5000 is the only miracle that's recorded in all four Gospels. John tells us that the multitudes were following Jesus hoping to witness something amazing. They were looking for a sensational demonstration of power. Jesus had been healing the sick, and the crowds were growing and growing, creating a real crowd-management problem. No concession stands had been set up. No vendors had been contracted to provide food. This had all the makings of a public relations disaster.

We can imagine how the excitement of the disciples—those closest to Jesus—must have been building as the crowds grew. They must have felt they were part of something really big, a movement that was gaining momentum. And then came the question, and with the question a foreboding sense of reality set in. Jesus turned to his disciples and asked, "'Have you thought about the food?'" (John 6:5). And just as suddenly as the excitement had built, it disappeared in the abrupt realization that several thousand people were hungry, restless, and agitated.

You know the story. Jesus, who paid taxes with a coin from the mouth of a fish, now turns to a box lunch that some Galilean mother had packed for her little boy. Andrew represents us in this story—all of us with our bodies heavy with doubt. "'Here is a boy,'" he said,

> *Jesus takes the ordinary things of this world, a few loaves and fish, and he reveals the extraordinary glory of God.*

"'with five small barley loaves and two small fish, but how far will they go among so many?'" (John 6:9). Nobody in this story can see beyond the wall of impossibility. The numbers, as we say, don't lie. There are 5000 men and only five loaves and two fish. And the fish are "small."

Jesus receives that bread from the little boy and he gives thanks. What was Jesus thankful for? Quite simply, he was thankful for the food, the physical bread that nourished his body. But Jesus was also thankful for the spiritual bread, the glory that was going to be revealed in him. Jesus takes the ordinary things of this world, a few loaves and fish, and he reveals the extraordinary glory of God.

Jesus was already looking ahead to the final act in the drama. He was looking ahead to another time when he would once again break bread, but this time in more intimate surroundings. Only hours before his death, Jesus was seated at a table in a small room in an ordinary home somewhere in Jerusalem. He took the bread and broke it, just as his body would soon be broken. "'Do this in remembrance of me,'" he said. We eat the bread, we drink the juice, and we reach out to lay hold of the wonderful Bread of Life. Two worlds are brought together in that moment—the physical bread that sustains us and the spiritual bread that saves us.

The Geography of Faith

Patrick wanted the window seat. There was nothing to see on an overnight flight that took us across Greenland, the North Sea, Finland, Russia, Turkmenistan, Pakistan, and finally India. But that's not why he wanted to sit there. He just wanted to sleep—and the window seat, along with Dramamine and Excedrin PM, offered him his best chance.

Instead, we talked.

We talked about the upcoming mission trip and the magic show he was going to perform in the village. We talked about the technical challenges of showing the *Jesus* film under the stars, surrounded by bamboo, banana trees, and rice fields. We talked about our families and our day jobs. We decided it would probably be best for Patrick not to tell the villagers what he did for a living, since their tribal religion included the belief in ghosts. We kept talking, and over the space of the next several hours—at least as far as southern Russia—I learned more than I ever wanted to know about the dark arts of embalming.

I thought back a few years to the first time I met Patrick. New to our church, he and his wife dropped in on our midweek home fellowship. We were going through the Gospel of John. On the very night they visited, we had come to the eleventh chapter. The story is plotted across the intersection of our existence—right at the juncture of body and soul. Lazarus, it turns out, was a man with a foot in both worlds. I remember when we reached the point in the story where Jesus said, "'Take away the stone'" (John 11:39). Martha objected. She knew a few things about the world; she knew how a dead body would smell after four days.

"I can verify what Martha is saying," Patrick said. "I'm a mortician. Bodies really do stink after four days."

How does faith survive grave clothes? We want to know what Lazarus saw, what he felt, what he experienced in the great beyond. What secrets could he reveal to us? He didn't have a Near Death Experience. *He actually died*—and came back four days later. What could he tell us? Did he see a bright light? Was there a tunnel?

But we learn nothing. John's Gospel is dead silent, so to speak, on the biggest question we have. This silence is powerful and eloquent. The Gospels refuse to indulge our curiosity. All we know is that Jesus stepped toward the grave. He lifted up his eyes and cried out in a loud voice. *Lazarus, come forth!*

In the village we dug the holes and planted the bamboo. We strung the sheet from end to end and pulled it tight. We cranked up the generator as day retreated to a thin orange ribbon in the west. Across the rice fields the water buffalo were lumbering home. The stars flickered into view. I watched a lone satellite crawl across an empty stretch of sky.

Our makeshift screen lit up with strange images drawn from the Gospel of Luke. I wasn't expecting the voice I heard. I'm used to Jesus speaking in a deep, sonorous voice, with a touch of a British accent, refined and restrained, every syllable carefully weighed. Instead, Jesus spoke in the tribal language of the Rajbanshi people, and his voice was high-pitched, nasally, and wholly unimpressive.

And yet the old women who crouched at the back of the crowd watched with rapt attention. They clucked their disapproval as Jesus was beaten and spit upon. And the little boys and girls gathered toward the front. The men lingered at the edges of the crowd, but they too were watching. And when the light shone into the empty tomb, everyone was silent.

There in a field on the edge of a little village in Nepal, with our feet planted in the dust and the bamboo poles anchored firmly in the ground, the Son of Man was lifted up once again above the earth.

That's always the geography of faith, because Jesus too had a foot in both worlds.

Summing-Up: Doubt is grounded in the world, but so is faith. Jesus taught his disciples to look around at the natural world and see God at work. Jesus called men and women to look beyond physical things to the spiritual truths that give them meaning. When we recognize that God is fully engaged in his creation, then we find ourselves halfway to faith.

For Further Reflection

1. Jesus spoke of the birds that God feeds. Do animals have faith? How are the behaviors of our pets similar to faith? How are they different?

2. If the Human Development Index (HDI) were applied to individuals, how would you rank? Would the HDI tell the whole story of your life? What would it leave out?

3. It's sometimes hard to see and hear God beyond the routines, schedules, and habits of our lives. How can we keep our faith vibrant when our feet seem so planted in the world?

4. If you were Nicodemus (John 3) or the Samaritan woman (John 4), would you have asked the same questions? What does this tell you about yourself? About faith?

PART 2

How We Believe

*"The LORD God...breathed into
his nostrils the breath of life."*

GENESIS 2:7 ESV

CHAPTER 8

Under a Fig Tree

Key Idea: Faith responds to the
smallest hints of God's goodness
in the world and in the Word.

JESUS BEGAN HIS MINISTRY IN THE SHADOW OF A FIG TREE. And since Jesus'
ministry was all about drawing men and women to a life of faith, this is a
good place for us to start too as we turn to the question, *How do we believe?*

John's Gospel describes the first few days of Jesus' public ministry. He
opens in dramatic fashion, taking us back to the eternal existence of Christ
as the Logos, the Word of God (John 1:1). John choreographs a dizzying, cosmic entrance for Christ before setting him down in an ordinary place by the
Jordan River. That's where John the Baptist saw Jesus and made his great confession, the one that introduced Jesus to the world: "'Look, the Lamb of God,
who takes away the sin of the world!'" (John 1:29).

John the apostle then tells us how Jesus called his disciples, picking them off
one by one. He called Andrew, and then Andrew told Peter. He called Philip,
and then Philip told Nathanael. And in the calling of these disciples we see
a little picture of how people have always been called to Christ—one by one.

Nathanael's Quiet Time

Philip must have run. He was probably out of breath by the time he
found his brother Nathanael sitting under a fig tree. Philip had an amazing,
even an unbelievable, announcement to make, and so he just blurted it out:

"'We have found the one Moses wrote about in the Law, and about whom the prophets also wrote—Jesus of Nazareth, the son of Joseph'" (John 1:45).

Philip's message can be reduced to a simple equation:

$$\{\text{the one Moses wrote about}\} = \{\text{a carpenter named Jesus}\}$$

No doubt the juxtaposition filled them with wonder and confusion. Faithful Jews like Nathanael knew that the Messiah would be a man (Deuteronomy 18:15); but to be confronted with the reality that he has a common name, comes from a provincial town, and is the son of a carpenter—this must have been too much to wrap their minds around. Nathanael gave a predictable response: "'Nazareth! Can anything good come from there?'" (v. 46). But in spite of his doubts, Nathanael went with his brother to meet Jesus.

> When Jesus saw Nathanael approaching, he said of him, "Here is a true Israelite, in whom there is nothing false."
> "How do you know me?" Nathanael asked.
> Jesus answered, "I saw you while you were still under the fig tree before Philip called you" (John 1:47-48).

What's so special about the fig tree? It's one of the common fruit trees of the Holy Land, but it's also a rich symbol of promise and expectation. The fig tree is a biblical picture of Israel—and bound up in the fragrance of the blossom, the sweetness of the fruit, and the coolness of the shade is the blessing of God.

The small homes in ancient Israel gave a man little privacy. There was no man cave, no finished basement, no converted garage. Often homes did have a roof where you could retire; but you usually had to go outside the home—to the shade of the fig tree—to find peace and quiet. The fig tree was a place to have your quiet time alone with God and meditate upon the law. As a faithful Jew, "in whom there is nothing false," this is probably what Nathanael was doing when Jesus saw him. Under the fig tree we find shade. We retire from the bustle of the home. We take in the fragrance of the blossoms above our head. This is the promise of God—the promise that there is much more than this, even though *this* by itself is a wonderful gift. We find promise there and hope; we experience the goodness of God. We find a little taste of what's to come. When Solomon reigned in Israel, the land was at peace with "every man under his vine and under his fig tree" (1 Kings 4:25 ESV). Solomon's reign is a miniature picture of the peaceable kingdom, the millennial reign of Christ on earth. This is what every faithful Jew was waiting for. Especially Nathanael.

Nathanael took hold of the promise of God in a tangible, "sensible" way. With one foot in the world of God's creation, he pivoted and stepped toward God by faith, declaring, "'Rabbi, you are the Son of God; you are the King of Israel'" (John 1:49). Jesus rewarded his step of faith with a sneak preview of coming attractions:

> Jesus said, "You believe because I told you I saw you under the fig tree. You shall see greater things than that." He then added, "I tell you the truth, you shall see heaven open and the angels of God ascending and descending on the Son of Man" (vv. 50-51).

Nathanael would have understood the reference. Jesus was taking him all the way back to a dream Jacob had, a dream of a ladder between heaven and earth (Genesis 28:10-22). That ladder was the point of contact between this world and the next, like a portal into the spiritual realm. Jesus was telling Na-

The heart that delights in God is the heart where faith can grow.

thanael, "I'm that ladder." You see, Jesus is the ultimate man with a foot in both worlds. He's both the Son of Man and the Son of God, and that's why he's the mediator, or the ladder, between man and God (1 Timothy 2:5).

Faith is waiting upon God as we sit under the fig tree enjoying the pleasure of his promises. David spoke much about "delighting" in the things of God.

> Delight yourself in the LORD
> and he will give you the desires of your heart.
> (Psalm 37:4)

This is what Jesus saw in Nathanael—a pure delight in the God who made all things good and gave us all things to enjoy. David's promise came true that day. Nathanael received the desires of his heart when he received Jesus.

The heart that delights in God is the heart where faith can grow. I know this because I see how God poured faith into my young heart. I look back and realize now that my faith too began under a fig tree.

Riding Concubines

The quaint word *devout* comes to mind when I describe my childhood. I was a missionary kid, an MK—not that this provided any guarantees about how I'd turn out in the end. I knew plenty of MKs who went bad; I was one of them for a while. Still, I see God's grace in allowing me to sit in the shade of my parents' faith and have a Bible placed in my hands at an early age. I acquired the vocabulary of faith, if not always the substance. God was forming within me the capacity to know him and to walk by faith. I guess the vocabulary had to come first—even if it was the archaic vocabulary of the King James Version.

When my parents went to Cleveland, Ohio, for a two-week missionary orientation, my brother and I stayed with Uncle Byron and Aunt Joyce. I vividly remember the outing we made into the wheat fields of Central Oregon. Two things stand out in my memory—how we rode a combine through the fields, and how I described it later to my parents. I gave them a hug and then excitedly announced the highlight of the previous two weeks. "I rode a concubine!" I said with a triumphant grin. Only a child who had grown up reading the King James Bible could possibly make such a claim.

I was a child who read the Bible—even with all the "thees" and "thous." Even with all the concubines. At an early age I developed a hunger for God's Word. I sat often under the fig tree. All this came back to me one day with a rush of memories when the two Bibles I read as a child were returned to me unexpectedly in the mail. They arrived like the three angels who visited Abram's tent on the Plains of Mamre. The whole thing was kind of ordinary, kind of unusual, but really significant in a way I understood only later.

We had left a lot of personal things in Africa. A missionary friend was kind enough to carry a few items home with her many years later, when the old mission compound was evacuated and abandoned. In that package were my first two "grown-up" Bibles—one red and one brown. I hadn't seen or held them for years. They fell into my hands like a spiritual time capsule, transporting me back to the dawn of my faith. As I thumbed through the pages and read my childish reflections, I took note of the strange patterns of my underlining and winced at my curious theologies.

But I also found some insights into the first awkward steps we make toward faith when we sit under the fig tree.

My Red Bible

I opened the box and took out the red King James Bible. I fanned the pages and a tiny handmade church bulletin fell out. Apparently, while other kids were manufacturing spit balls in the pews, I was designing miniature bulletins that listed me as "Pastor Babcock." The message I was going to deliver, according to the bulletin, was "God Knows Every Secret Thing."

I kept flipping through the leaves of the Bible. Written into the white space between Malachi and Matthew I found my first sermon—on the story of Jonah, with snatches of Noah thrown in. Written at the top of the page was the declaration: "I am Planning on being a Preacher when I get old." And then, as though to seal my reputation at eight years old as a hellfire-and-brimstone preacher, I emphasized the judgment of God. "There's Going to be more People in Hell than Heaven," I wrote. "Their were Less People in the Ark than out."

It felt strange to open this Bible and recreate my adolescent thinking. As a graduate student, I was trained to read medieval manuscripts, decipher annotations, and interpret glosses. Now I was turning those techniques of literary and textual criticism on myself.

My critical eye discerned, for example, the fingerprints of a fundamentalist background—not that I needed an advanced degree to figure that out. It was pretty obvious. My notes displayed a youthful tendency to draw out, wherever possible and with relentless detail, the consequences of God's judgment. For instance, in 1 Samuel 12:25 Samuel warned Israel not to rebel against God: "But if ye shall still do wickedly, ye shall be consumed, both ye and your king." That was my cue to jot down in the margin, "consumed in hell," just to make sure it was perfectly clear what God was talking about.

The idea of the "fear of God" particularly resonated with me as a child. I had underlined 1 Samuel 11:7—"And the fear of the LORD fell on the people, and they came out with one consent." Again, I fixed upon the conditional phrase in 1 Samuel 12:14, "If ye will fear the LORD." I understood the fear of God in relation to my role as a child. I was to show God the same respect due to my parents and their beliefs. That's why I underlined Proverbs 30:17—"The eye that mocketh at his father, and despiseth to obey his mother, the ravens of the valley shall pick it out, and the young eagles shall eat it."

It would be easy for me to see this as a "deformed" faith, one that neatly fits the caricatures of those who throw stones at Christianity. Fear of God,

> *One of the great tragedies of modern Christianity is the failure of parents to pass on to their children a real and vital faith.*

eternal judgment in hell, ravens picking out the eyes of disobedient children. Looked at a certain way, it's pretty scary.

In fact, many who grew up in a Christian home as I did have abandoned their faith as adults. This is one of the great tragedies of modern Christianity—the failure of parents to pass on to their children a real and vital faith that connects them to the past and prepares them for the future.

Many lapsed Christians look back at their childhood faith and see deformity. But I don't see a deformed faith at all, but an *unformed* faith. Ultimately, the goal of faith is to be *conformed* to the image of God's Son. Paul describes it this way.

> And we know that in all things God works for the good of those who love him, who have been called according to his purpose. For those God foreknew he also predestined to be conformed to the likeness of his Son, that he might be the firstborn among many brothers (Romans 8:28-29).

Paul realized that it was a difficult project to be conformed to Christ. It involved labor, work, discipline, and consistency. In one of his earliest letters, Paul told the Galatians that "I am again in the pains of childbirth until *Christ is formed in you*" (Galatians 4:19, emphasis added). I now see the good work that God was always doing as he formed faith in the heart of a child.

My young faith wasn't just about hellfire, brimstone, and the fear of God. There in the scorched earth of God's judgment, I recognized a few green shoots of God's grace. First Samuel 12:24 pulled all these themes together—and I underlined that verse too: "Only fear the LORD, and serve him in truth with all your heart: for consider how great things he hath done for you."

It would be many years before I would come to a fuller understanding of the depths of that verse and its tragic irony for King Saul. But already at age eight God was working faith into my heart. Like Saul, I would walk away from God's calling. But God never took his Spirit from me the way he did with Saul. He would draw me back.

In addition to those verses that spoke of the fear of God and his judgment, I underlined Jeremiah 15:16, another green shoot of God's grace: "Thy words were found, and I did eat them; and thy word was unto me the joy and rejoicing of mine heart: for I am called by thy name, O Lord God of hosts."

That's the key—the skeleton key, really, to how faith is formed in our lives. Faith pivots around the words that God has spoken to us. Creation resonates with the deep undertones of his voice. We hear him too through the very human, very simple words that are stitched together as the 66 books of Scripture. These are the words of an unformed faith, yearning toward its Object, waiting like Nathanael for the substance—even if that substance has a name like Jesus and comes from a town like Nazareth.

My Brown Bible

I took my second grown-up Bible out of the box. It was brown, and it was the first Bible I read from cover to cover. As I thumbed through the pages, I saw four distinct tendencies in my markings and marginalia.

First, my notes were often little more than elementary glosses on the verse. I would add a few words to bring out the obvious meaning, in a way that seems completely unnecessary to me now. For example, where 1 Thessalonians 3:5 reads, "lest by some means the tempter have tempted you," I wrote "Satan" in the margin, as though it wasn't already perfectly clear. Where Galatians 6:17 reads, "I bear in my body the marks of the Lord Jesus," I added the words, "suffered with him." Where 1 Thessalonians 5:10 reads, "whether we wake or sleep we should live together with him," I found it helpful to add the words, "for eternity."

This seems to me now a rather childish level of interaction with the Bible. It would be easy to dismiss it as such. But I see a faith step in this which I'll call *learning to rename simple things*—that is, drawing out the basic meanings and stating the obvious.

In 2 John 8, the phrase "that we receive a full reward" seemed obscure enough to me then to merit my helpful clarification, "in heaven." Yes, a reward should make me think of heaven. And no, it's not just a place I name as a child—a place that exists because I believe in it. It's not some flannelgraph figment of my childish imagination. I must continue to rename it, just as I did then. I begin as a child by renaming simple things and restating simple truths, but I must continue to do that. Paul never stopped saying the obvious: "Now there is in store for me the crown of righteousness, which the Lord, the righteous Judge, will award to me on that day—and not only to me, but also to all who have longed for his appearing" (2 Timothy 4:8).

Paul hasn't gotten over this "childish" notion of heaven. He's not graduated into some kind of existential man who has "suffered the loss of all things" (Philippians 3:8 ESV) for nothing more than the claim of personal vindication and integrity. Paul meant it when he wrote in 1 Corinthians 15:19 that we are the most miserable of men if we cling to a hope that fizzles when we die. Paul doesn't say, "we have a different kind of hope." He says we'd have *no hope at all* if Christ didn't rise from the dead—if it isn't *true*, if it isn't *real*. Paul restates, and reaffirms, simple things.

My brown Bible revealed a second tendency—to notice patterns, see repetitions, and make connections. In Ephesians 4:4-6 I circled "one" seven times. I noted the contrast in Ephesians 4:22-24 between the "old man" and the "new man." Next to James 2:26 I scribbled down the observation that this was the third time James stated that "faith without works is dead." I was beginning to grasp that faith is not some unstructured, amorphous *feeling*. It's as orderly as the sentences I found in Scripture.

This led naturally to my third tendency—the systematic outlining of passages. Galatians 6:9, for example, seemed to fall into three parts for me, which I conveniently alliterated.

A command ("And let us not be weary in well doing")

A comfort ("for in due season we shall reap")

A condition ("if we faint not")

Of course, I was imitating the homiletic style I heard from a Baptist pulpit. But I was also approaching the Bible as something that made sense, something that communicated truth in a clear and organized way, and something that could be applied to our lives.

And that was my final tendency—to apply God's Word. And here's where I see the forming of my faith most clearly, especially in the marginalia that I wrote next to this verse: "For thus saith the Lord God, the Holy One of Israel: In returning and rest shall ye be saved; in quietness and in confidence shall be your strength: and ye would not" (Isaiah 30:15).

I had written the date and place into the margin. "Feb. 24, 1975, Monday, Dorm, Crampel, Central African Republic." I was 12 years old and living several hundred miles from my parents in a missionary boarding school. Now, as an adult, I deciphered the cramped notations that stretched around the margins of page 585. The story, which I had long forgotten, came back to me.

> *We just got word here at the dorm that there would be no mid-term break because of the epidemic at Ippy. I needed something to hold on to. I asked the Lord to show me something.*

I noted that I had already read and marked this passage once before, but had never yet applied its truth to my life.

> *The brackets in light blue around the verse were placed there before, but they had no meaning. But as I read this chapter for the third time (this was my 3rd time thru the Bible), the verse stuck out, especially "And ye would not." This verse gave me strength. I had been trying on my own strength to be happy despite the fact that we weren't having mid-term break. Now I see that the "Holy One of Israel" brings the joy.*

I had a long way to go in the forming of my faith. I had many years of sojourning in Egypt ahead of me. But God had breathed into me the breath of life, and he had poured into me the God-breathed Word of life. Holding these Bibles in my hands and leafing through their pages, I was reminded that we cannot separate God's Word from the life of faith, since "faith comes by hearing, and hearing by the word of God" (Romans 10:17 NKJV).

We cannot separate God's Word from the life of faith.

The fingers of an invisible God had molded my faith. His thumbs pressed out the cavities of my ears so I could hear his voice. He shaped the sockets of my eyes so I could see his mighty works. Unless God does this work, we are deaf and dumb and blind, like the idols we make and worship.

Madeleine Cakes and Fig Trees

Smell and taste are the only senses that have a chemical basis, which is why they're such powerful carriers of memory. Catch a whiff of something and you can instantly be transported back to a distant time and place. Scientists claim that these must have been the first of our senses to evolve, since they imagine life emerging from a primordial soup of chemical interactions. But here's what

I think. God wants to remind us that we can never reach beyond this world until we first grasp the goodness of God right here, right now.

One of the great works of twentieth-century literature begins with a taste and a memory. *Remembrance of Things Past* is a novel about memory—seven volumes of memory, to be exact—and it begins with the taste of Madeleine cakes. Marcel Proust writes of how this traditional French sweet cake could summon up in his memory all the good things of his childhood. One taste, and it was Sunday once again in his aunt's kitchen where the cakes were soaking in lime blossom.

I'm sure Nathanael would have understood this. Every time he smelled the fig trees in blossom, he must have remembered that first encounter with Christ. The first stirring of faith begins with the scent of fig blossoms in the air—with our embrace of the goodness of God. This is where faith *must* begin, since faith has feet of clay.

But as faith grows, deepens, and strengthens, it will inevitably lead us and sustain us in a world that is gray, desolate, and barren. A world where trees don't blossom in springtime. Where flowers droop and die for lack of water and the birds can no longer feed their young. What happens to faith, then?

The prophet Habakkuk had an answer. He knew that it's not enough for faith to be grounded in the world. Faith must ultimately reach toward the knowledge of our Creator or it never becomes fully formed. It remains stunted and is not really faith at all but something pointless and self-contained, lacking an ultimate object. A faith that has grown to maturity should last even when the fig tree withers.

> Though the fig tree does not bud
>   and there are no grapes on the vines,
> though the olive crop fails
>   and the fields produce no food,
> though there are no sheep in the pen
>   and no cattle in the stalls,
> yet I will rejoice in the LORD,
>   I will be joyful in God my Savior.
> The Sovereign LORD is my strength;
>   he makes my feet like the feet of a deer,
>   he enables me to go on the heights.
>   (Habakkuk 3:17-19)

So this is our journey. We know what kind of land we're traveling into. We have to expect long stretches with no service stations—kind of like driving into the Mojave Desert. But God "knows how we are formed, he remembers that we are dust" (Psalm 103:14). Because we're dust, because we're made of minerals and chemical compounds, we can catch the scent of blossoms on the wind and conjure the taste of Madeleine cakes—simple delights the angels will never experience. Because of this, we can *remember,* and we can hope.

God knows that we need to see and experience his goodness. Once we've smelled the fig tree or tasted its sweet fruit, we're ready to trust and follow him. All of Scripture is an invitation to experience the goodness of God. This invitation comes to us, for example, in the form of a love poem written by Solomon, where the fig tree appears one more time.

> The fig tree forms its early fruit;
>   the blossoming vines spread their fragrance.
> Arise, come my darling;
>   my beautiful one, come with me.
>
> (Song of Songs 2:13)

The early Church Fathers heard the voice of allegory in this, and so should we. This is the invitation to follow Christ. We must plant our foot in this world of fig trees and blossoms, lilies and turtledoves—and turn in the direction of his voice.

"Come my darling; my beautiful one, come with me."

Summing-Up: Faith has humble beginnings. We start with a foot planted in this world of sense and experience and pivot toward God. We find hints and echoes of God's promises in the good things of this world. We take small steps and learn to hear his voice in Scripture. That's how God grows our faith as we begin to trust in his goodness.

HOW CAN I BELIEVE WHEN I HAVE SO MANY DOUBTS?

For Further Reflection

1. Where were you when Christ first called you? How did you hear his voice? Was there a Philip who introduced you to Christ?

2. Think back to your first childish steps of faith. What did your faith look like then? What was unformed about your faith?

3. What is the "fig tree" in your life that you retire to? Is there a place where God's presence and promises seem more tangible to you?

4. How important has the Word of God been in the development of your faith?

CHAPTER 9

First Things First

Key Idea: Genuine faith rests on a
foundation of first principles—the
belief that God is real and good.

TRUTH IS ALWAYS FOUND IN THE BOTTOM DRAWER.

In one of Norman Rockwell's most endearing recreations of middle-class, mid-twentieth-century American life, we see a young boy, maybe six or seven, standing next to his father's dresser. The bottom drawer has been pulled out, and the little boy is standing there in his pajamas, his back to the dresser, his mouth wide open in astonishment, his eyes as round as saucers. Then you see what he's pulled out of the dresser, what's still clutched in his hands and falling around his feet—a red suit with white trim.

I grew up indifferent to Santa Claus. My parents never pretended he was real. We never left cookies and milk by the fireplace on Christmas Eve. So when I stood watching the jolly man himself ride by outside our

*Doubt doesn't
have to reduce our
world to rubble.*

home on some motorized vehicle, lights flashing, Christmas music blaring from a flatbed truck, I viewed him—even at age six—with classical detachment. But I've had my moments of disillusionment. I've opened the bottom drawer on more than one occasion. My eyes too have turned into saucers.

Doubt doesn't have to crush us. It doesn't have to reduce our world to rubble. Yes, I want a childlike faith, since this is what Jesus told me I should have. But I don't want a *childish* faith. I want to know what is true. Jesus spoke of this kind of faith, and we've been puzzled ever since by what he meant.

> At that time the disciples came to Jesus and asked, "Who is the greatest in the kingdom of heaven?" He called a little child and had him stand among them. And he said: "I tell you the truth, unless you change and become like little children, you will never enter the kingdom of heaven. Therefore, whoever humbles himself like this child is the greatest in the kingdom of heaven" (Matthew 18:1-4).

Faith isn't even mentioned in these verses, so where do we get the notion of childlike faith? "'Unless you change,'" Jesus said, and "'humble yourselves like this child.'" Faith, if that's what Jesus is speaking about, requires a change in how we live. It requires that we stop relying on ourselves and place ourselves instead under the control of our heavenly Father.

Yes, Virginia

How exactly do we "become like little children"? I don't want to settle for some fairy-tale form of believing despite everything my head tells me about the world. *Yes, Virginia, there is a Santa Claus—and, by the way, there's a God too.* After all, this is what Christianity's most vocal critics claim about us—that we close our eyes and retreat into a childish, feel-good escapism that we call faith.

Jesus would have rejected that out of hand. When he brought a child before his disciples and said, "Believe like this," he wasn't suggesting that we should stop asking questions or searching for answers. Jesus must have intended for us to do exactly the opposite—to ask a lot of questions, loads and loads of them, one right after the other, since that's what children do.

Who made God?

Where do pets go when they die?

Why do bad things happen to us?

These questions are asked without cynicism. The child, unlike the lawyer, is not building a case question by question. There's no "gotcha moment" at the end of the interrogation.

Take Virginia, for example, who asked a famous question in 1897. She took her question to her daddy, who promptly passed the buck by suggesting she write to the anonymous editorial board of *The New York Sun.* For many, the response that Virginia received is a warm affirmation of faith and goodness. For others, including myself, it's a cynical exercise in how fantasy can masquerade as faith.

The letter and the famous response by Francis Church have become a canonical part of our Christmas lore.

> DEAR EDITOR: I am 8 years old.
> Some of my little friends say there is no Santa Claus.
> Papa says, "If you see it in THE SUN it's so."
> Please tell me the truth; is there a Santa Claus?

Francis Pharcellus Church was a staff writer for *The Sun.* His obituary described him as "a sardonic and cold-blooded" commentator on controversial issues. Reportedly, he was less than enthusiastic when given the task of writing a response to an eight-year-old girl on the weighty and pressing subject of Santa Claus. Still, he produced a minor masterpiece.

> Virginia, your little friends are wrong. They have been affected by the skepticism of a skeptical age…Yes, Virginia, there is a Santa Claus. He exists as certainly as love and generosity and devotion exist, and you know that they abound and give your life its highest beauty and joy…Nobody sees Santa Claus, but that is no sign that there is no Santa Claus. The most real things in the world are those that neither children nor men can see…Nobody can conceive or imagine all the wonders there are unseen and unseeable in the world.

Why did Church's reluctant essay achieve the status of a classic? The clue lies in the phrase "the skepticism of a skeptical age." This was Church's skepticism too. This is why Church's short essay struck a chord that hasn't stopped resonating over a hundred years later. Santa Claus had become a placeholder for God. It didn't really matter anymore whether Santa Claus or God even exists. *What matters is that we believe.*

James Barrie, the author of *Peter Pan,* gave expression to the same sentiment. The story of the boy who didn't want to grow up debuted on stage in London around the same time, in the early 1900s, before appearing as a novel in 1911. The secret to flying, Peter explained, was faith. Or as he put it, "All you need is faith and trust and a little bit of pixie dust!"

Santa Claus and Peter Pan—these are modern faith fables. But the kind of faith they model is nothing like the faith of Abraham and Elijah. It's a faith that says, "I really hope so," or "I'd like to believe that," or "I think the world's a better place if we close our eyes, hold hands, and wish." Faith is not viewed as something rigorous, substantial, sturdy. Instead it's a wispy, fragile thing, like butterfly wings. It's viewed as childish. Pixie dust—that is, fantasy and imagination—are more important than trust. According to this view, which is held by the most sophisticated minds of our age, we all have our divine placeholders. If not Santa Claus or Peter Pan, then maybe some New Age myth that "isn't true" but is "meaningful" nonetheless.

> *Our faith and everything we believe must rest on something foundational— a set of first principles.*

Pajamas and Paradigms

So we come back to the question: *How can I believe when I have so many doubts?* It should be clear that we don't believe *like this*. We don't believe because it makes us feel good or because it's therapeutic to look on the bright side, to see the good in people and always hope for the best. We don't believe because it makes the world a better place if we trust in fairies and angels and Santa Claus and God. When we open the Bible, we want to know that we're encountering real people with real experiences about a real God who really loves us.

At the base of our doubts is the nagging fear that we'll pull open that bottom drawer and find a God-suit all folded up with nothing inside. Here's where knowing what's in the bottom drawer is essential. Our faith and everything we believe must rest on something foundational—a set of first principles.

The little boy in Rockwell's painting is standing agape and desolate in his striped pajamas. His world has shifted on its axis before the day has even started. Like Alice in Wonderland, he had believed "seven impossible things before breakfast"—and now all of them were shattered by the opening of a single drawer. He doesn't know it, but this little boy in pajamas is undergoing what is sometimes called a "paradigm shift."

What is a paradigm? It's a framework of understanding, a structure set up to answer questions and solve problems. The word is a technical term used to describe the grammatical sets we learn when studying grammar.

I sing	we sing
you sing	you sing
he, she, it sings	they sing

That's a paradigm; it tells you that the verb "to sing" changes depending on who is doing the singing. The paradigm tells you what to do when you want to say "he" or "she" with the verb "sing." You've got to remember to add the *s* to the verb. So a paradigm is a structure that gives you answers. Question: *How do I conjugate the verb "to sing"?* Answer: *Add* s *in the third person singular.*

In 1962, a physicist at Harvard University, Thomas Kuhn, took this well-established word out of the field of linguistics and used it as his way to describe "systems of thought," "ways of looking at problems." In his highly influential book, *The Structure of Scientific Revolutions,* Kuhn considered how paradigms shape our understanding of the world. They provide the conceptual framework through which we ask questions and find answers. Paradigms are necessary to scientific thinking, Kuhn argued, since we must always start with a grid of interlocking assumptions.

But what happens when your paradigm is flawed? The prevailing cosmological paradigm of the ancient and medieval worlds was geocentric, which means the earth was believed to be the center of God's creation. But Copernicus turned the paradigm on its head. He observed the physical data, calculated the figures, and determined that we'd been wrong all along. The earth is a planet that revolves around the sun. The old geocentric paradigm had been replaced by a new paradigm, the heliocentric or sun-centered model.

One of Thomas Kuhn's main points was that paradigms do, in fact, shift. The case of Copernicus demonstrates how science advances as old theories are discarded in light of new discoveries. Paradigm shifts occur in the spiritual realm as well. People do go from faith to unbelief, just as others are converted from unbelief to faith in God. A paradigm shift happens when we surrender our first principles—when we come to believe that they no longer explain the reality of what we experience or observe around us.

The opening verses of Hebrews 11 give us a faith paradigm, an unshakable

> *The opening verses of Hebrews 11 give us an unshakable set of first principles to ground our lives upon.*

set of first principles to ground our lives upon. This is the great "faith chapter" of the Bible, where we find Scripture's most sustained answer to our questions about faith and doubt. One by one we read of the men and women, the "ancients" whose lives were shaped by the reality of God, the truth of his presence, and the fact of his goodness. The central argument of Hebrews 11 is that these men and women of faith refused to swap out the really big things they knew about God for the relatively small things they didn't know about their daily lives.

The whole parade of heroes opens, like Church's editorial on Santa Claus, with a philosophical preamble.

> Now faith is being sure of what we hope for and certain of what we do not see. This is what the ancients were commended for.
> By faith we understand that the universe was formed at God's command, so that what is seen was not made out of what was visible...
> And without faith it is impossible to please God, because anyone who comes to him must believe that he exists and that he rewards those who earnestly seek him (Hebrews 11:1-3,6).

If you drill down to the bedrock of faith, you'd find these core convictions resting beneath all we believe. That's our faith paradigm. Two propositions, two first principles, make up this paradigm: *God is real* and *God is good.* As we read through Hebrews 11, we see that this really is how faith—as a paradigm—is presented to us. It's a governing structure for life, one that transcends the hows and whys of the moment through an immovable conviction that God is really there and he desires nothing but good for you and me.

The Reality of God

First, we must believe that God is. Despite the increasingly fashionable status of atheism in the Western world, the Bible is clear in its assertion that anything but belief in an all-powerful God is foolishness. "The fool says in his heart, 'There is no God'" (Psalm 14:1).

The Bible doesn't set out to prove God's existence; it merely assumes that God is a self-evident truth, an innate idea, a necessary logical assumption. It's *unnatural* not to believe in God. Paul didn't debate the point with the philosophers on Mars Hill (Acts 17:22-31), but accepted God's existence as the first predicate in his argument.

The Hebrew word, *nabal,* which is usually translated "fool," doesn't mean knave or dummkopf or chucklehead. It refers instead to a man who tries to live as though God isn't interested in his life. He's a thoroughly carnal, materialistic man. He doesn't necessarily deny the *reality* of God as a philosophical idea, but he rejects the *relevance* of God in practical experience. The fool, the *nabal,* lives as though God is an indifferent and uncaring no-show in the moral universe.

Nebuchadnezzar, the king of Babylon, was a *nabal*—a practical atheist. Daniel tells us that as Nebuchadnezzar walked on the roof of his palace and gazed upon Babylon, he exulted in the work of his hands (Daniel 4:30). As potentate, he had no room for God. His words spoke life and death to thousands.

But God humbled him and brought him to his senses: "He was driven away from people and ate grass like cattle. His body was drenched with the dew of heaven until his hair grew like the feathers of an eagle and his nails like the claws of a bird" (Daniel 4:33).

And then we read the confession of Nebuchadnezzar:

> At the end of that time, I, Nebuchadnezzar, raised my eyes toward heaven, and my sanity was restored. Then I praised the Most High; I honored and glorified him who lives forever.
>
>> His dominion is an eternal dominion;
>>> his kingdom endures from generation to generation.
>> All the peoples of the earth
>>> are regarded as nothing.
>> He does as he pleases
>>> with the powers of heaven
>>> and the peoples of the earth.
>> No one can hold back his hand
>>> or say to him: "What have you done?"
>
> (Daniel 4:34-35)

The story of Nebuchadnezzar teaches that belief in God is a necessary part of a truly rational framework of thinking.

The Bible simply doesn't waste its time with those who reject what we are preprogrammed to believe. I guess that's why I was so unimpressed after the first lecture in an apologetics course I once took in graduate school. The foundational lecture in the course was the Kalam cosmological argument for the existence of God. The history of the argument takes us back to medieval Baghdad—a great period of Islamic scholarship when *kalam,* the Islamic discipline of philosophy, flourished. The argument itself is expressed in the form of a classical syllogism, a three-pronged argument.

An actually infinite number of things cannot exist.

A beginningless series of events in time entails an actually infinite number of things.

Therefore, a beginningless series of events in time cannot exist.

Got it? Me neither. In the presentation and defense of this argument, one must eventually get around to defining infinite sets, quantum mechanics, the concept of imaginary time, and what medieval Arabic philosophers in Baghdad typically did on Wednesday afternoons. Well, not entirely, but you get the point.

> *Some things lie infinitely beyond our calculation. The existence of God is one of them.*

It's great mental gymnastics for somebody who actually thinks that way. But I remember my reaction as I plodded through the lecture. *How absurd,* I thought. *Can God really be reduced to this?* Must we go back to a medieval philosopher in Baghdad named al-Ghazli and work through mathematical intricacies just to establish what should be considered a self-evident truth? This "proving" that God exists must amuse God very much.

Some things lie infinitely beyond our calculation. The existence of God is one of them. This is the first principle for faith because nothing in the world makes sense apart from God. When I accept that God is, then I'm acknowledging that there's more to this life than what my mind can grasp and my senses can perceive. That's a significant first step.

The Goodness of God

Most people sense intuitively the foolishness of denying some sort of Higher Power. The question then becomes, *What kind of God is he?* Does he play with thunder like Zeus? Is he a shape-shifter like Vishnu? Is he force and energy? One billion people worship a remote and angry being named Allah. Is this who God is? Or is he the God revealed to us in the Bible?

The second principle of faith given in Hebrews 11:6, "that he rewards those who earnestly seek him," is a statement about God's nature. What kind of God is he? The Bible tells us that he is personal and he is good. He rewards those who seek after him. We can grasp this principle from the fact and fabric of creation, but it must be tested through experience. Paul pressed this message when he debated the philosophers in Athens. God can be found, he asserted, since "he is not far from each one of us" (Acts 17:27). When Paul preached in Lystra, he challenged those who worshipped Jupiter and Mercury by pointing to the goodness of God in creation: "'Yet he has not left himself without testimony: He has shown kindness by giving you rain from heaven and crops in their seasons; he provides you with plenty of food and fills your hearts with joy'" (Acts 14:17).

> *Faith is about placing our lives, our future, our hopes, our treasures into someone else's hands.*

This principle is crucial to the life of faith since faith is all about commitment and trust. Faith is about placing our lives, our future, our hopes, our treasures into someone else's hands. When we go into the voting booth, we commit ourselves *in faith* to the character of the man or woman we're casting our ballot for. Pollsters understand the power of this intangible dynamic, and so they try their best to probe our gut-level response to the candidates. They want to find out who we're ready to commit ourselves to. Often pollsters will ask a question that goes something like this: "Who would you want to join you at your backyard barbecue on a Saturday afternoon?"

Consider this for a moment. You wouldn't want to invite any of the gods of the ancient world to your barbecue. In fact, you wouldn't want them anywhere near your neighborhood. Most of the Greek gods, for example, would be listed on the Sex Offender Registry. The gods of the Canaanites were even worse. Molech, in particular, would be a really bad choice to join you for a barbecue. You wouldn't want him anywhere near the fire, as his idea of a barbecue begins and ends with your children. The pagan gods were thoroughly wretched beings.

The kind of God we believe in matters very much, since what we believe will determine how we live. If our God is hateful and vengeful, then there is little hope that our lives can be any better.

Jesus came to reveal to us that the Father in heaven is a personal God who is good. He entered into the homes of ordinary people and broke bread with them. He "went around doing good" (Acts 10:38). Jesus taught that God is deeply engaged in his creation, so much so that "even the very hairs of your head are all numbered" (Matthew 10:30).

The goodness of God is one of the great themes of Scripture, repeated from Genesis to Revelation. All the heroes of faith listed in Hebrews 11 suffered trials and reversals of fortune. But they were men and women of faith because they clung to the truth that God is good in all he does, whether we can see it or not.

This is a hard, rocky place in the road for most Christians. We can forget that sin has messed up this world, and now we have to live with the consequences of our rebellion against God. Sometimes the circumstances of life will stretch to the breaking point our human ability to understand God's goodness. That was the case with Job.

So how do we handle our doubts about the goodness of God?

First, *we shouldn't confuse the badness of circumstances with God's character.* From where Job sat—in sackcloth and ashes—there was nothing good in what had happened. He had lost his children, his crops, his health, and his dignity. But Job was faithful, which literally means that he "kept faith with God." He refused to retreat into the black hole of nihilism, the dead end of materialism. "Though he slay me," Job said, "yet will I hope in him" (Job 13:15). He would not join those carnal men who think God is irrelevant and indifferent.

True faith has muscles, sinews, joints, and tendons. It reaches out and lays hold of God.

Job didn't retreat from God either. He was willing to tell God how bad things were and how rotten he felt about it. God expects this kind of candor from us. He can take it. "'I will surely defend my ways to his face,'" Job said. "'Indeed, this will turn out for my deliverance, for no godless man would dare come before him!'" (Job 13:15-16).

Second, *we should never forget that God operates according to a cosmic blueprint we're not able to read.* We can't unfold his plans on the kitchen table, since God's blueprint stretches out beyond the galaxies. God's timetable is eternity itself.

> For he chose us in him before the creation of the world to be holy and blameless in his sight. In love he predestined us to be adopted as his sons through Jesus Christ, in accordance with his pleasure and will (Ephesians 1:4-5).

In other words, God knows what he's doing. And what he's doing is very good.

Responding Like a Creature

It's not enough for us to affirm intellectual truths about God, no matter how essential they are. James, the brother of Jesus, reminded us that "even the demons believe" (James 2:19). We might add that theologians also believe, and a lot of good people do too. But that kind of belief is not enough. It must be put into practice. It must be exercised. True faith has muscles, sinews, joints, and tendons. It reaches out and lays hold of God. It stretches its legs and runs toward the finish line.

These first principles are important. Faith isn't possible apart from this foundation. But a greater goal lies before us—a personal relationship with the living God. The writer of Hebrews, whoever he was, follows up his philosophical statements about God with a record of trust—a record of men and women who tested the boundaries of faith and proved God faithful.

Right knowledge must lead to a right response within us, a proper orientation of our heart toward God. As we contemplate all that God is, how should we respond? With wonder and humility. Both of these are creaturely responses to a Creator God. Wonder is the foundation of inquiry, and humility is the foundation of worship.

Wonder is amazement, a kind of speechless gazing beyond what is sensible and predictable into a world I cannot fully take in. Aristotle opened his greatest work of philosophy, *Metaphysics,* with this observation: "It was through the feeling of wonder that men now and at first began to philosophize." Aristotle's own puzzlement led him to explain things in terms of a Prime Mover, a First Cause that got the cosmic ball rolling. Children too possess wonder in abundance. We tend to lose it as we grow up. Poets and scientists and a few eccentrics find new ways to nurture the ancient awe, but most of us get jaded and cynical along the way. Christians are no exception, and that's a shame since we have so much to wonder at.

When David looked at the heavens he wondered, "What is man that you are mindful of him?" (Psalm 8:4). The fact that God *is*—the sheer weight of that idea—presses itself upon our mortality. What would David say if he could see the Hubble photographs that image deep space for us? Layer upon layer of galaxies, pinwheels, and clusters. Gaseous clouds in shades of purple and green. The majesty is overwhelming.

> *When we accept, as a precondition of all human thought, that we have limitations, then we have freed our hearts to wonder.*

David also wondered at the goodness of God. He wondered "What is man?" when he looked at creation. But he also wondered, in a more personal way, "Who am I?" when he considered God's call upon his life. David had felt the presence of his Creator as he stood beneath the starry host tending sheep. But there was more he would come to learn of God. Nathan the prophet brought an incredible promise to King David, telling him that his descendants would sit on an eternal throne (2 Samuel 7:12-13). How did David respond? He was blown away, gobsmacked, speechless. Scripture is more artful and restrained in its description, but we get the impression of a man who is completely at a loss for words. Wonder and humility overwhelmed him as he sat before the Lord (2 Samuel 7:18).

True wonder is inseparable from humility. If a scientist tackles the unknown as just another province of knowledge to be conquered, then he's given up on wonder. He's merely pounding down white picket fences of rational thought and carving out little rectangles of space that he controls. When we accept, as a precondition of all human thought, that we have limitations, then we have freed our hearts to wonder. Humility is not optional, as Albert Einstein seemed to recognize. "The human mind," he wrote, "is not capable of grasping the Universe."

> We are like a little child entering a huge library. The walls are covered to the ceilings with books in many different tongues. The child knows that someone must have written these books. It does not know who or how. It does not understand the languages in which they are written. But the child notes a definite plan in the arrangement of the books—a mysterious order which it does not comprehend, but only dimly suspects.

Consider how one of the great minds of the Middle Ages, Anselm of Canterbury, humbled himself before his Creator. Before Anselm presented his great ontological argument for the existence of God, before he laid out this elegant monument to rational thought, he wrote a prologue in the form of a simple, childlike prayer.

> I acknowledge, O Lord, with thanksgiving, that thou hast created this thy image in me, so that, remembering thee, I may think of thee, may love thee. But this image is so effaced and worn away by my faults, it is so obscured by the smoke of my sins, that it cannot do what it was made to do, unless thou renew and reform it. I am not trying, O Lord, to penetrate thy loftiness, for I cannot begin to match my understanding with it, but I desire in some measure to understand thy truth, which my heart believes and loves. For I do not seek to understand in order to believe, but I believe in order to understand. For this too I believe, that "unless I believe, I shall not understand."

I am not trying to penetrate thy loftiness. Anselm got it right. We seek "in some measure" to understand God, but we also know our limits.

David got it right too. He understood, and confessed, his limitations. He acknowledged his dependence upon God.

> My heart is not proud, O Lord,
>   my eyes are not haughty;
> I do not concern myself with great matters
>   or things too wonderful for me.

> But I have stilled and quieted my soul;
> like a weaned child with its mother,
> like a weaned child is my soul within me.
>
> (Psalm 131:1-2)

Wonder and humility. When we lose these, we gradually lose even the ability to believe.

Opening the Envelope

One of the twentieth century's great theologians was a humble German preacher who wondered much about God. Helmut Thielicke described doubt as an envelope with a message inside. He understood that doubt can be productive when it motivates us to open the envelope, with wonder and humility, and receive God's revelation.

Faith isn't strengthened by laying out our arguments but by laying down our lives and abandoning ourselves to the promises of God.

In his book *A Little Exercise for Young Theologians,* Thielicke distilled the many years of wisdom he had gained in the pulpit, not the seminary. He counseled young theologians to "do theology" in the second person, as he put it, not the third person. The grammatical distinction between "you" and "he" changes everything when we reflect upon God. Our reflections should be prayerful, a humble dialogue addressed to God, whom we speak of as "you." Instead our theology is usually intellectual, directed to one another; we speak of God as "he," as though he's in another room—or in another galaxy, for that matter.

It's a simple but brilliant insight from a preacher who saw the ravages of World War II from inside Germany. He saw the corrosive impact of fascism upon the church. Thielicke witnessed compromise and spinelessness; he knew that we desperately need to direct our theology toward God in prayer if theology is to have any value in such a world. Men such as this remind me that faith isn't really bolstered by reason but by risk. Faith isn't strengthened by laying out our arguments but by laying down our lives and abandoning ourselves to the promises of God.

The life of faith calls us to practice these truths—not just to hold them as intellectual postulates but to live them out radically in our lives. Do I live as though God is real? Do others see that I am trusting in a good God whose goodness does not depend upon the changing circumstances of life? Do I talk *to* God or do I talk *about* him?

No other apologetics—no logical argumentation about the existence of God—will carry more weight than the simple conviction of a life lived with the certainty that God is real, God is present, and God is good.

Summing-Up: The foundation of faith in God is the belief that he is real and he is good. These first principles must govern the life of faith. It's not enough, however, to believe in God as a philosophical idea. God has revealed himself to us so that we may know him personally as we approach him with hearts filled with wonder and humility.

For Further Reflection

1. From your experience, how would you say the world views faith? How is it characterized or caricatured? Does it matter whether what you believe is true or not?

2. Do you have more difficulty with the existence of God or the goodness of God? Why?

3. What things in the natural world produce the greatest sense of wonder in you?

4. Why is humility necessary to true faith in God?

CHAPTER 10

The Mainspring of Life

Key Idea: Faith is God's central
power source for salvation
and the Christian life.

ONE OF THE GREAT ICONS OF THE CHRISTIAN FAITH, the Victorian preacher Charles Haddon Spurgeon, described faith as a choice we make. "Faith then, we choose, rather than doubt, as the mainspring of our life." Spurgeon wasn't making a theoretical observation. He was describing his own life, his own wrestling with doubts, his own conviction that we ultimately exercise our will toward God. Spurgeon knew this to be true because he made that choice one snowy winter day. Just as significantly, he *continued* to make that choice each and every day, despite the doubts and struggles that dogged him throughout his life.

Some 280 times, in the thousands of sermons he preached between 1854 and 1892 at the Metropolitan Tabernacle in London, Spurgeon told the same story of how he came to faith in Christ. He never embellished it. He never pumped it up the way some evangelists do when telling their testimonies. It simply was what it was. Spurgeon related the story most fully in his autobiography.

> I sometimes think I might have been in darkness and despair until now had it not been for the goodness of God in sending a snowstorm one Sunday morning while I was going to a certain place of worship. When I could go no further I turned down a side street and came to a little Primitive Methodist Chapel.

There were no more than 15 or so people in the congregation. Spurgeon had heard about the Primitive Methodists and how "they sang so loudly that they made people's heads ache." But the despondent teenager set his biases aside. "I wanted to know how I might be saved," Spurgeon wrote, "and if they could tell me that, I did not care how much they made my head ache."

The minister wasn't there, perhaps because of the snow, and "at last a very thin looking man, a shoemaker or tailor or something of that sort, went up into the pulpit to preach." The man stammered, didn't pronounce his words correctly, and "was obliged to stick to his text for the simple reason that he had little else to say." He spoke for only a few minutes on a single verse, which he read out of the King James Version: "Look unto me, and be ye saved, all the ends of the earth" (Isaiah 45:22).

Spurgeon would go on to become one of the most celebrated preachers in church history, but the sermon he heard that day was far from a textbook example of the art of homiletics. Still, the summary of this humble sermon must rank among the clearest definitions of faith ever given.

> My dear friends, this is a very simple text indeed. It says, "Look." Now lookin' don't take a deal of pains. It ain't liftin' your foot or your finger; it is just, "Look." Well, a man needn't go to College to learn to look. You may be the biggest fool, and yet you can look. A man needn't be worth a thousand a year to be able to look. Anyone can look; even a child can look. But then the text says, "Look unto Me." Many of ye are lookin' to yourselves, but it's no use lookin' there. You'll never find any comfort in yourselves.

And then "the shoemaker or tailor or something of that sort" brought his message home with a personal appeal. He was looking directly at the young Spurgeon.

> "Look unto Me; I am sweatin' great drops of blood. Look unto Me; I am hangin' on the cross. Look unto Me; I am dead and buried. Look unto Me; I rise again. Look unto Me; I ascend to Heaven. Look unto Me; I am sittin' at the Father's right hand. O poor sinner, look unto Me! Look unto Me!"

"Oh! I looked," Spurgeon wrote, "until I could almost have looked my eyes away."

There and then the cloud was gone, the darkness had rolled away, and that moment I saw the sun; and I could have risen that instant, and sung with the most enthusiastic of them, of the precious blood of Christ, and simple faith which looks alone to Him.

Simple faith—that's what Spurgeon chose that day when he looked at Jesus.

Faith Keeps on Ticking

Throughout his life Spurgeon would continue to struggle with doubts and anxieties. He passed through many seasons of depression. But the simple faith that God gave him that day proved to be sufficient. He would continue to "choose faith, not doubt, as the mainspring of life."

When he wrote those words, I'm sure Spurgeon was thinking of the watch that hung from a chain and rested in his pocket. Powered by a tightly wound metal coil called the mainspring, the watch had to be wound up each day if it was going to keep everything else in order.

We would think instead of a wristwatch, though few of us have to wind up our watches anymore. My first watch was a simple, indestructible, no frills, windup Timex. That was back in the 1960s when one out of every two watches sold in the United States was made by the Middlebury, Connecticut, manufacturer of mechanical watches. During those years the Timex slogan was, "It takes a licking and keeps on ticking." That's a pretty good description of faith too, as Spurgeon could testify.

In one magazine ad, Mickey Mantle was shown with a Timex watch taped to his baseball bat. The caption read: "Unusual Verified Shock Test Proves Timex Can Take a Licking Yet Keep on Ticking." In another ad that appeared in the *Saturday Evening Post,* boxer Rocky Marciano pounded a punching bag with a Timex strapped to his wrist. Timex watches deserved their reputation; they were made to be durable. But the mainspring, which is common to all windup watches, is the real marvel of strength.

What is a mainspring? It's an ingenious invention, a little technological wonder. The simple mainspring, when wound up, compresses and stores a great amount of energy that is then released incrementally over time. This remarkable miniaturization of power revolutionized the art and science of keeping time.

Nowadays, most watches are powered by batteries or even the sun, and

Spurgeon's metaphor has become increasingly remote to us. Still, the main-spring is a subtle metaphor that points us to three great truths about faith.

- Faith is the central power source for the spiritual life.
- Faith holds tremendous energy in reserve.
- Faith must be wound up daily in order to be effective.

Walk Like This

First, *faith is the central power source for the spiritual life.* We are saved by faith, but we also live by faith. Even a casual reading of Paul's epistles will lead us to this conclusion.

> For it is by grace you have been saved, *through faith* (Ephesians 2:8).

> The righteous shall live *by faith* (Galatians 3:11).

> We have gained access *by faith* into this grace in which we now stand (Romans 5:2).

> We live *by faith,* not by sight (2 Corinthians 5:7).

Why is faith God's mechanism of choice both for salvation and godly living? Because faith takes us outside and beyond ourselves. It forces us to lay hold of the spiritual realm and reach out toward all we were created to be. To deny faith is to deny God's ultimate intention for us.

We are saved by faith, but we also live by faith.

One of the great struggles of practical Christianity is our failure to connect the moment of conversion with the unfolding moments of our lives. Paul saw no disconnect between how we first come to Christ by faith and how we are to follow him: "Therefore, as you received Christ Jesus the Lord, so walk in him" (Colossians 2:6 ESV).

Paul establishes a simple equivalence that's expressed by the words *as* and *so.* He's saying that we walk in Christ *the same way* we first received him. How did we receive Christ? By faith. We're told to walk like this. We don't come to the cross by faith and then walk away in the power of the flesh. From beginning to end, we're called to the self-emptying task of committing ourselves fully to the promises of God.

Christians have always struggled with this. Paul rebuked the Galatians, in what was probably the first letter he wrote, for trying to live by works and not by faith.

> You foolish Galatians! Who has bewitched you? Before your very eyes Jesus Christ was clearly portrayed as crucified. I would like to learn just one thing from you: Did you receive the Spirit by observing the law, or by believing what you heard? Are you so foolish? After beginning with the Spirit, are you now trying to attain your goal by human effort? (Galatians 3:1-3).

Nothing is a bigger faith-killer than trying to live a godly life in the power of the flesh—apart from the Spirit and apart from the nurturing power of God's Word. *We just can't do it.* And when we fail, as we surely will, we often blame God for what our own sorry efforts have produced.

Faith alone, like a mainspring, regulates the entire mechanism of our lives with precise consistency. It's the central element that makes all the gears tick. It's not just one part among many; it regulates the whole thing. Faith is sometimes wrongly viewed as one element among many in the Christian life. It is, rather, the one great principle that we must learn, since "without faith it is impossible to please God" (Hebrews 11:6).

If faith is so central, then how should we understand 1 Corinthians 13:13? Paul writes, "And now these three remain: faith, hope and love. But the greatest of these is love." We can't pluck this verse out of context and reduce Paul's theology to "Love makes the world go round." We're not justified by love, so clearly love is not greater than faith in the matter of our salvation (Romans 4:3). We walk by faith (2 Corinthians 5:7), so clearly love is not greater than faith in the matter of our Christian life, either.

First Corinthians 13:13 has become something of a Catholic prooftext for responding to the *sola fide* doctrine ("by faith alone") of the Reformation. Martin Luther's conversion and ultimate break with Roman Catholic theology turned on his rediscovery of the doctrines of faith and grace. It's not by works that we are saved. It's not by the sacraments of the church. It's through faith in Christ alone.

Peter Kreeft, a leading Catholic apologist and philosopher, has interpreted

1 Corinthians 13:13 to mean that faith, hope, and love operate equally in the salvation of our souls: "Faith is the root, the necessary beginning. Hope is the stem, the energy that makes the plant grow. Love is the fruit, the flower, the visible product."

This is a beautiful way to visualize faith, hope, and love. And it's an accurate way to describe how Scripture presents the trajectory, from beginning to end, of God's complete work of salvation in us. But that's not what Paul is talking about.

So what is Paul saying? In what way is love greater than faith? Paul is not speaking here of salvation but of the operation of spiritual gifts within the Body of Christ. In a lengthy exposition that stretches over several chapters, Paul is correcting abuses of the charismatic gifts in the Corinthian church. By the time we get to chapter 13, the so-called "love chapter," Paul has been discussing the gifts already for a chapter or two. Chapter 13 is a parenthesis, really, in his exposition on the proper exercise of tongues and prophecy.

We cherry-pick this chapter, as we do with so many other parts of Scripture, with little regard to how Paul intended it to be read. There are, of course, universal applications to what Paul says about love; and there's nothing wrong with having the chapter read as part of a wedding ceremony. But we should not try to develop a theology out of 1 Corinthians 13:13 that is at odds with everything else Paul says in the epistles. *In the matter of spiritual gifts*, Paul says, *love is superior to faith.*

> *Faith regulates everything because it's the point of contact between all that we are and all that God has intended for us to be.*

We need to set aside our muddy thinking and affirm the biblical status of faith. Nothing displaces faith, not even love, as the central power source of the Christian life. Faith is the necessary element, the critical component; life with God is not even possible without it. Faith regulates everything because it's the point of contact between all that we are and all that God has intended for us to be.

Mustard Seeds and Morning Milk

Faith holds tremendous energy in reserve—that's the second great truth we see. Faith is what justifies us before God. It's what gives us access to the Father. Faith is not some soft, willowy emotion, a function of the imagination—as in Neverland where all you have to do is "believe." Faith is a dynamic force. It transforms lives. It moves mountains.

Watch repairers know the power of a mainspring. It is wound so tightly and stores so much energy that it can even be dangerous. It can cut flesh, cause blindness, or rip apart the mechanism of the watch. Fortunately, we don't have to wear leather gloves and cover our eyes with goggles when it comes to faith. But faith too stores a tremendous amount of energy that we barely tap into.

Faith is so potent, so concentrated, that it takes just a little to save us. The story is told of a drunkard in the late nineteenth century who was saved from a dead-end life on skid row when, at the depth of his desperation, he came to understand one simple thing: *He had no power to save himself.* In his drunken state, he could do nothing but fall toward the cross. And that's what he did. He became an evangelist, bringing that simple message of faith to thousands in the Bowery district of New York. How much faith—how much power or energy—is required to come to God? Just enough to fall toward the cross.

> *The one who multiplies loaves and fish can take the little faith that I have and multiply it too.*

Growing in Christ means learning how to tap into the vast reservoir of spiritual power available to us only through faith. We start with enough faith to fall forward. Soon we're able to stand up in faith (Romans 5:2), walk in faith (2 Corinthians 5:7), and even run by faith (Hebrews 12:1). Perhaps nobody in the modern church has illustrated the progression of faith more than the nineteenth-century evangelist and humanitarian George Mueller. One morning in an orphanage in Liverpool, England, the breakfast table was empty. The pantry was empty. The money jar was empty. George Mueller looked at the hungry children, lifted his hand, and prayed, "Lord, we thank you for the food we are about to eat." Just then there was a knock at the door and the baker, who said he couldn't sleep all night, gave them a fresh batch of bread. A second knock at the door brought the milkman whose wagon had broken down in front of the orphanage. "The milk will spoil unless you use it," he said.

I confess I don't understand this kind of faith. If there were a Richter scale for faith, this would register off the chart. But even Mueller tapped into a very small portion of God's power. That's why I'm encouraged by what Jesus said to the disciples: "'I tell you the truth, if you have faith as small as a mustard seed, you can say to this mountain, "Move from here to there" and it will move. Nothing will be impossible for you'" (Matthew 17:20).

Faith this small is not much faith. It's approximately what I can muster. But the one who multiplies loaves and fish can take the little faith that I have and multiply it too.

Yes, a mustard seed of faith is enough; but God always requires us to act on the faith we have. This is why Jesus rebuked the disciples ("'O you of little faith'") when they were tossed about in a storm (Matthew 8:26 ESV). The disciples quickly reverted to type—burly, muscle-bound fisherman leaning hard into the oars, attempting to save themselves. The disciples saw the tremendous power of the wind and waves and forgot the infinite power available through faith.

The Routines of Faith

Just like the mainspring in a watch, *faith must be wound up daily in order to be effective.* Faith is a powerful resource given to us by God, but all this power lies dormant if we don't wind it up and actually use it. It must be exercised and maintained. We must put faith into action if it's to remain functional in our lives.

So how do we wind up our faith?

James would have been comfortable with Spurgeon's description of faith as "the mainspring of life." His short epistle is the most practical book on faith ever written. Nothing else even comes close. That's why we can turn to James as a resource manual for the practical exercise of faith.

Some have proposed that James wrote his letter to Jewish Christians very early, as soon as 15 years or so after the Resurrection. That would make it one of the earliest New Testament books. There does seem to be something "primitive" about James that captures the essence of early Christianity. We hear many echoes of Jesus sprinkled throughout the epistle. We don't see the full development of a systematic Christian doctrine that we find in Paul's later writings.

And James seems unaware of Gentile Christians, which may point to the earliest period when Christianity was still viewed as an offshoot of Judaism.

James may therefore be a window into the earliest, formative years of the Christian church. And that interests me, because James has much to say about faith. Right from the start of the church, we see that faith was a central idea—though the way James defines faith has proved controversial.

The main theme of James is that "faith without deeds is useless" (James 2:20), or "dead" in the familiar language of the King James Version. Martin Luther, the greatest figure of the Reformation, struggled with James and the message that seems, on the surface at least, to run counter to Paul's clear teaching on justification by faith alone. Paul could hardly be clearer when he wrote that "no one will be declared righteous in his sight by observing the law" (Romans 3:20). So how do we reconcile James and Paul?

Let's start by looking more closely at what James meant. Though James speaks much of faith, he's not really answering questions about doubt, skepticism, or unbelief—all those things we normally set opposite to faith. Rather, he contrasts faith with hypocrisy, lack of authenticity, deadness, and formalism. As modern rationalists, we tend to limit our definition of faith to "belief." We focus on all the intellectual questions we have, as though this is faith's greatest challenge. But James would have little sympathy for our handwringing over philosophical problems.

A faith that fails to match up words with deeds is an inauthentic, unsettled, and immature faith.

The greatest obstacles to faith in the ancient world were idolatry and hypocrisy. A first-century Christian would have faced relentless questions and ridicule for rejecting what "everybody knows is true," namely, that there are many gods. "Maybe Jesus is a god too. Or maybe he's the offspring of one of the gods. But how preposterous to claim that he is the *only* God!" James is telling the first Christians that if they really believe in one God, then they should live consistent with that belief.

Our approach, as modern rational Christians, would be very different. We'd write books laying out the unbeliever's case and demolishing each argument one by one. We'd stage public debates with the worshippers of Jupiter. That's because we're preoccupied with challenges of the mind.

James doesn't see faith that way. Instead, he downgrades intellectual questions to a single, narrow area of what believing is all about: "You believe that there is one God. Good! Even the demons believe that—and shudder" (James 2:19). My loose paraphrase goes like this: "Good for you for believing that God exists! I'm not even going to argue the point. So go ahead and congratulate yourself. The demons are right there on the same page with you!"

The early Christians didn't cast faith primarily in opposition to intellectual doubt; rather, they saw true faith in contrast to hypocrisy. James addresses this right from the start of his letter when he writes about the man who asks God for wisdom.

> But when he asks, he must believe and not doubt, because he who doubts is like a wave of the sea, blown and tossed by the wind. That man should not think he will receive anything from the Lord; he is a double-minded man, unstable in all he does (James 1:6-8).

On a first reading, it appears that James is contrasting faith with doubt as you and I ordinarily do. That is, we must believe—without a single doubt—that God can and will answer prayer. But the emphasis in this passage, as throughout all of James, is on *authentic* Christianity. We are to seek God's wisdom, not our own, and when we do that we should look to God and not the things of this earth. Being double-minded is alternating between two worlds—the two worlds our feet are planted in. This is not so much a *doubting* faith as it is an inauthentic, unsettled, and immature faith—a faith that fails to match up words with deeds.

James follows closely the teaching of Jesus. Both defined faith as "spiritual authenticity." We are told to be authentic toward other people (2:9-10), to meet the needs of people with genuineness and generosity (2:15-16), to be real and transparent in our speech (3:1-12), to establish sincere and loving relationships with others (4:1-11), and to have no ulterior motives when making long-range plans (4:13-15).

About halfway through his letter, James comes back to wisdom. And here's where we find the key.

Who is wise and understanding among you? Let him show it by his good life, by deeds done in the humility that comes from wisdom. But if you harbor bitter envy and selfish ambition in your hearts, do not boast about it or deny the truth. Such "wisdom" does not come down from heaven but is earthly, unspiritual, of the devil. For where you have envy and selfish ambition, there you find disorder and every evil practice.

But the wisdom that comes from heaven is first of all pure; then peace-loving, considerate, submissive, full of mercy and good fruit, impartial and sincere (3:13-17).

Wisdom is knowing how to live God's way; and this is a spiritual, not a fleshly, attribute. We can acquire this kind of wisdom only by faith, since faith pushes us toward the spiritual and away from the fleshly. This is the authentic spiritual life, as contrasted with a fleshly life that is bound in the grave clothes of a dead formalism.

So how do we reconcile James and Paul?

Luther couldn't see the harmony here, but there's no fundamental disagreement. Paul always presents doctrine from God's perspective, and this is true of faith as well. James is anchoring faith in the church, in the concrete demonstration of something that is real in the heart. Faith, for James, is something as real as a comforting touch, a cup of water when you're thirsty, food and clothing for the widows and orphans, oil on the head of the sick and dying.

We've seen the importance of having the right first principles, of believing that God exists and that "he rewards those who earnestly seek him" (Hebrews 11:6). And we saw the importance of responding to God with wonder and humility. But what next? James tells us. Now go pursue the life of faith. Actually do it. Throw yourself into it. Wind up the mainspring.

"But I can't stop asking these questions!"

Fine. Pat yourself on the back for having creaturely questions about your Creator, and then put your hand back on the plough and start living in obedience to God. When you choose to settle down into doubt, then you're not advancing in the life of faith. Don't dismiss your questions—but don't make your dwelling there. Paul didn't. Spurgeon didn't. They kept advancing toward the goal, toward "the high calling of God in Christ Jesus" (Philippians 3:14).

Summing-Up: Faith is the central mechanism God uses to accomplish his work in us. We are saved by faith and we are called to live by faith each day. James teaches that faith is genuine only when it is expressed through our lives. Faith must be put into action; it must be exercised through choices that take us beyond the wisdom of this world.

For Further Reflection

1. How does your watch regulate your life? Does faith regulate your spiritual life the same way?

2. Has there ever been a time in your life when you were called upon to exercise great faith? Where did your faith come from? Describe what happened.

3. Does the world view faith or love as more important? How would you respond with a biblical answer?

4. Can you have works without faith? Can you have faith without works? Give an example of each from your life.

CHAPTER 11

How Faith Is Built

Key Idea: Faith is always nurtured
and expressed within the community
of believers, the church.

WEEK AFTER WEEK, USUALLY AFTER DINNER, we'd pile into the van, cruise down the expressway, drive up Old Forest Road by the Honda dealership, turn left onto Link near the Dairy Queen, ease into a subdivision, and finally head up a dead-end street. We would arrive at an undeveloped lot, get out of the car, and look at nothing.

It took a few months for our builder, a self-described "good old boy" named Ned, to get started. We kept waiting for heavy equipment to appear on the property. We waited for brambles and vines, shrubs and trees to succumb to the crushing advance of civilization, for the faint outline of a driveway to emerge from the red clay.

It takes patience and imagination to build a house. When the work finally began, the progress was slow. Dense underbrush had to be bulldozed and burned. The land needed grading. But gradually we had something to look at, something to do on our weekly pilgrimages. Wesley and Mary clambered among piles of dirt, stacks of bricks, and heaps of gravel as Janel and I called after them rather pointlessly, the way parents do, "Don't get dirty!"

We tried to imagine where the living room or dining room would be—"between this rock and that ant hill"—and we began arranging the furniture before the foundation was even poured. Even the deer were wondering about things. We arrived at our future address one day to find a small herd standing in the middle of our property. They seemed confused; this used to be their private forest. All of us were adjusting.

Building a house is also about decisions. Ned and I walked off the dimensions of the house, put down some stakes, stepped back to look at it again, and then moved the stakes 10 feet closer to the road. Every time Janel and I sit on the front porch and watch the sun drop below the mountains at dusk, we enjoy a view made possible by that extra 10 feet. We made some good decisions.

We were never meant to be freelancers in the life of faith.

Faith is built like this—with patience, imagination, and good decisions.

Building a house is one of the ways Scripture describes to us the life of faith. Curiously, the picture seems out of sync with the imagery of tents and pilgrimage. So which is it? Are we pilgrims living in tents? Or are we settling down, laying a foundation, and building a house?

We're both—and there's no contradiction.

Mixed Metaphors

We were never meant to be freelancers in the life of faith, but to live out faith within a community of believers. Peter describes us as "living stones" fitted together and built up "into a spiritual house" on the foundation of Christ (1 Peter 2:5). A stone by itself is worthless. But when joined together according to a divine blueprint, the stone becomes something beautiful, something capable of bringing glory to God.

Paul uses a variety of metaphors when he writes, and he does this too when describing the church. In his letter to the Ephesians, Paul describes the church as a building (2:20-22), a bride (5:32), and a body (1:22-23). But whatever metaphor he uses, Paul consistently describes the church as a place where our faith is to be nurtured and then expressed. We are to grow in faith and then show that faith in word and deed. Anything falling short of this twofold objective—nurturing and expressing faith—is a deviation from the biblical template for the church (Ephesians 4:11-16).

The early Christians understood this. One of the distinguishing features of early Christianity was its reputation within the Roman Empire as a close-knit community. Even the pagan Romans noticed that Christians stuck together. They genuinely seemed to love one another; and even when they didn't, they learned to love each other anyway by the grace of God. They knew they had only each other. If you were a Christian in Rome or Antioch or Jerusalem, then you didn't have any other place to go if you didn't like the color of the carpet or the style of worship or the pastor's sense of humor. You were either *in* the community or *out*. You could thumb through the Yellow Pages all you wanted to and explore your options. But you had none.

"What are we?" Tertullian asked in the second century. "A body compacted by a community of religion, of discipline, and of hope." This early Church Father was replying to accusations, lies, and propaganda directed against the early church. In so doing, he appealed to the virtues of the Christian community—the way believers gathered for prayer and exhortation, the way they took voluntary donations to help the poor and suffering in their midst. How did pagan Romans see this? Tertullian tells us that it was viewed as a mark of weakness. "See how they love one another!"

All the secularists of the modern Western world had better thank their lucky stars (or whatever pagans believe in nowadays) that Christian ethics, not Roman ethics, prevailed in the end. The Romans starved and abandoned their unwanted infants. For entertainment they tortured the weak and powerless in public forums. They chopped the limbs off runaway slaves. Meanwhile, Christians loved one another. Which kind of Western world would you rather live in?

How do we measure up to the love test? This is the great standardized test of true Christianity (John 13:35). You see, our values as a community are critical to our faith. If there is no distinction between the community of believers and the community at large, then how can my faith be nurtured? Wouldn't my "faith"—if we could even call it that—be just as well served by joining a gym or a tennis club? We've lost the sense of desperation that binds us together—and our love and faith have suffered as a result.

The Lost Community

The Greek word *koinonia* is used by the New Testament writers to describe this unique bond of Christian fellowship. Though the word is usually translated "fellowship," it really means something much richer and deeper than that. It means participation, investing myself in others, so that their fate becomes my fate. It means breaking bread—the bread of a potluck, the bread of Communion, and the bread of God's Word. *Koinonia* means "communion," holding things in *common,* which is the basis of every community. And what is the basis of our community if not our profession of faith?

This idea of community is expressed in the most ancient formulation of church doctrine, the Apostles' Creed, as the *communio sanctorum,* "the communion of saints." It's found right after the phrase, "I believe in the holy catholic church." Christians, like myself, who did not grow up reciting the Apostles' Creed find these phrases sticking in our throats. We have to learn that "catholic" doesn't refer in this context to a church hierarchy based in Rome; it means the *universal* church, the spiritual church, the Body of Christ. The phrase "communion of saints" must be understood the same way—as a fellowship of believers that transcends the boundaries of time and space.

> *American evangelicals love the idea of community but seldom embrace its reality.*

A Christian community, then, is framed around *doctrinal,* not *demographic,* features. We're not just another community, like the "shrimp fishing community," or the "model airplane hobbyist community" or the "gay/lesbian/transgendered community." None of these are communities in any meaningful sense of the word. They are designations of demographic units. Modern Western Christians tend to bring the secular culture of identity politics to the community of saints, forgetting that the *communio sanctorum* is invisible, mystical, and is comprised of every believer, living and dead, in heaven and in earth, regardless of whether they speak English and vote Republican. Here's the bottom line: *The communion of saints is bigger than us.*

American evangelicals love the idea of community but seldom embrace its reality. We want community on our terms. We have so many churches to choose from that we've developed a new social behavior, nearly unique to American Christianity—the practice of "looking for a church." Books have been written to help walk you through the process, but the very notion of "looking for a church" would have puzzled most Christians throughout church history.

With the blood of pioneers and homesteaders flowing in our veins, we're individuals to a fault. We want a designer faith that meets the narrow criteria of our likes and dislikes. We see this in how the church is marketed—especially our megachurches where volunteers in parking lots serve us coffee and donuts while we wait for the next shuttle to the sanctuary.

Too often these churches create a community in name only, giving the illusion of connectedness while carefully maintaining the kind of distance—the "on my terms" level of involvement—that Americans seem to expect. We want the freedom to opt in or opt out whenever we decide. Any stronger level of commitment looks somewhat cultish to us.

By design, megachurches can appear to be vibrant and thriving hubs of faith. Many are even called "community churches." But there can be something transient, superficial, and ultimately cynical about a community of faith that's created through dramatic reenactment—sound systems, spotlights, PowerPoint sermons, and donuts in the parking lot. This is church for a mobile lifestyle, but it's not the kind of mobility that Abraham, that dweller in tents, would have recognized.

The answer to this faux community is not to force Christians out of the suburbs into small country churches with steeples and wooden pews. The answer is not to proliferate small groups and home fellowships as a counterbalance to the "big church" experience. The answer is not to atomize our ministry such that we have Bible studies for every conceivable census category. The answer, I'm afraid, is to make it harder, not easier, to be a part of the community. We do this not by excluding people but by defining the community around the central propositions of our faith.

While I was writing this chapter, an e-mail popped up in my browser from one of the megachurches in my area advertising the start-up of small groups on Wednesday nights. Not surprisingly, they're called "community groups," and they're built up around interests and needs—"a great opportunity for you and your friends to learn a new skill or develop an existing one." You can join together with others of similar interest and learn to sew, scrapbook, and make jewelry. You can get genealogical tips for "figuring out your family tree." GED preparation and fibromyalgia support are available, as well as financial planning and English as a second language. The list goes on with martial arts and oil painting, photography and golf. There's even a class—a single class—on witnessing, if that happens to be your cup of tea.

When you translate this into the context of the early church, a rather preposterous, even grotesque church emerges. Imagine a community group for ex-slaves headed up by Onesimus and offering support for those transitioning to a new stage of their life (Philemon 10-17). Timothy could lead a very sensitive and timely support group for Gentile Christians who have undergone circumcision (see Acts 16:1-3). Of course, Dorcas would be the natural leader of the sewing group (Acts 9:36-41).

> *The church is not primarily designed to meet our social needs. It's designed to nurture and nourish our faith.*

My contention is that it's harder to believe, not easier, when we define community in the world's terms. A true community of believers, the communion of saints, is held together not by common political views or demographic features, not by hobbies or interests. The communion of saints is always sustained by faith. There's nothing intrinsically bad about community groups such as these, but we can easily forget that the church is not primarily designed to meet our social needs. It's designed to nurture and nourish our faith within the context of a common confession.

Most books that deal with faith and doubt, including this one, treat it as a very personal thing. But faith has a collective dimension to it as well. Both the Old and New Testaments speak clearly about this. David wrote:

> I will give you thanks in the great assembly;
> among throngs of people I will praise you.
> (Psalm 35:18)

The early church too understood that collective worship was the great incubator of faith:

> Every day they continued to meet together in the temple courts. They broke bread in their homes and ate together with glad and sincere hearts, praising God and enjoying the favor of all the people. And the Lord added to their number daily those who were being saved (Acts 2:46-47).

We can focus so much on the individual experience of faith that we neglect this vital corporate dimension. *How can I believe?* A big part of the answer lies not in better arguments but in a stronger community. After all, we speak of *faith* when describing both our personal relationship with God and our collective relationship through the Body of Christ. Paul wrote to the Romans that "we maintain that a man is justified by faith apart from observing the law" (Romans 3:28). Jude urged the early church "to contend for the faith that was once for all entrusted to the saints" (Jude 3). The same Greek word, *pistis,* is used in each verse to describe a faith that is both a personal affirmation and a corporate declaration.

I remember wading across a small stream to reach a primitive little village in rural Nepal. There was a small church there, a humble building made of bamboo and a thatched roof. "How many believers are here?" I asked. "Seven houses," was the answer. This is the typical way that the size of a fellowship is described in Nepal. In the United States we count heads. We count how many seats are occupied in the sanctuary. Nepali Christians are closer to the biblical model. They count homes and families. As Paul said to the Philippian jailor, "'Believe in the Lord Jesus, and you will be saved—you and your household'" (Acts 16:31).

A failure of faith is often a failure of community—at least in part. We're ultimately responsible, of course, for the choices we make as individuals. For example, Demas labored side by side with the great apostle Paul for many years, but in the end he bailed out. "Demas has forsaken me," Paul wrote in his final letter, "having loved this present world" (2 Timothy 4:10 NKJV). Gehazi was Elisha's servant and personal assistant for many years, and yet he too embraced the empty promises of this world (2 Kings 5:20-27). No one had more light and more opportunity than Judas, but he gave up the Kingdom of God for 30 pieces of silver. It was his choice.

These colossal failures don't change the fact that faith was always meant to be nurtured within a body of believers. Many times when Christians fall by the way, there's been some

> *Every generation of believers has a responsibility to interrogate its faith statements by laying them side by side with Scripture.*

breakdown in how the community has nurtured and encouraged their faith. I think of

- every young Christian whose questions and doubts have never been answered with candor and sensitivity
- every hurting Christian whose wounds have never been tended to with love and concern
- every Christian who has been victimized by legalism and judgment, hypocrisy and manipulation

These are all faith killers. And even when faith is not killed, it's often stunted and deformed. The purpose of the church, Paul tells us, is "to prepare God's people for works of service, so that the body of Christ may be built up until we all reach unity in the faith" (Ephesians 4:12-13).

A Baptist Sermon

The metaphor of a building is a powerful, process-driven way to think about faith. It's a biblical image, first used by Jesus: "'And I tell you that you are Peter, and on this rock I will build my church, and the gates of Hades will not overcome it'" (Matthew 16:18).

We always build from the foundation up; there's no other way to do it. Then we frame the building so that the rooms, doorways, and windows take shape. Finally, we finish it with the molding and fixtures, window treatments and paint. And just like that we have a building—as well as a Baptist sermon with three alliterated points.

- The foundation speaks of being *confident* in our faith.
- The framework speaks of being *complete* in our faith.
- The finishing speaks of being *comfortable* in our faith.

First, our faith is built on a foundation. Abraham "was looking forward to the city with foundations, whose architect and builder is God" (Hebrews 11:10). This speaks of *being confident* in faith, steady and certain about essential things. One of the reasons it took so long for our house to be built was the solid rock that lay just beneath the surface. Our house was built on a rock—literally.

What is our foundation as believers? When answering that question, we should go straight to the Bible—not to our creeds or doctrinal statements, not to our denominational distinctives. Every generation of believers has a responsibility to interrogate its faith statements by laying them side by side with Scripture. This is the only way to make sure that culture and tradition have not been grafted into our faith.

Let's go back to Matthew 16, since this is a foundational text in every sense of the word:

> "But what about you?" [Jesus] asked. "Who do you say I am?"
> Simon Peter answered, "You are the Christ, the Son of the living God."
> Jesus replied, "Blessed are you, Simon son of Jonah, for this was not revealed to you by man, but by my Father in heaven. And I tell you that you are Peter, and on this rock I will build my church, and the gates of Hades will not overcome it" (Matthew 16:15-19).

What is the rock? What is the foundation? The confession that Jesus is the Son of God—this is the foundation of the church.

Paul links this confession to the historical fact of the Resurrection, since the Resurrection confirms who Jesus truly is: "Who through the Spirit of holiness was declared with power to be the Son of God by his resurrection from the dead: Jesus Christ our Lord" (Romans 1:4).

At the heart of this statement is the same confession that Peter made. Paul constantly brought these two confessions together—*that Jesus is the Son of God and that he rose from the dead*—when he explains what it means to be saved: "That if you confess with your mouth, 'Jesus is Lord,' and believe in your heart that God raised him from the dead, you will be saved" (Romans 10:9).

The New Testament couldn't be any clearer about the foundation of our faith. If we build on anything else, then we're building on sand (Matthew 7:26).

After the foundation is established, the building is framed. This speaks of *being complete* in faith. The rooms are marked out. The space is designated. When our house was being built, it was exciting to be able to walk through the framework of rooms and hallways as they began to take shape. We walked up and down the steps to the second floor. We walked down the hallway and into rooms through the outline of walls. The house wasn't complete yet, but it was *becoming* complete.

As important as the foundation is, it's only the beginning of the work. Paul reminds us that Christ is our foundation (Ephesians 2:20), but he goes on to say that there's a work that God is building on that foundation of Christ, our cornerstone: "In him the whole building is joined together ["fitly framed" KJV] and rises to become a holy temple in the Lord. And in him you too are being built together to become a dwelling in which God lives by his Spirit" (Ephesians 2:21-22).

> *The greatest mystery of all is that we are in Christ—and Christ is in us.*

As we grow in faith, we learn that we are "complete in him" (Colossians 2:10 NKJV). We also learn that Christ's completeness is inexhaustible. We'll never come to the end of *becoming complete.* Christ solves the basic problem first posed by Job, and it's one of the most basic problems of faith. We looked at this passage earlier, in light of the transcendence of God. Now let's look at it again as a description of the great building project that God is doing in us.

> "Can you fathom the mysteries of God?
>   Can you probe the limits of the Almighty?
> They are higher than the heavens—what can you do?
>   They are deeper than the depths of the grave—
>   what can you know?
> Their measure is longer than the earth
>   and wider than the sea."
> (Job 11:7-9)

How can the creature know his Creator? Like Job, Paul takes out his tape measure and calculates the dimensions. But Paul is measuring the house that God is building through Christ—the house that you and I move into by faith.

> I pray that out of his glorious riches he may strengthen you with power through his Spirit in your inner being, so that Christ may dwell in your hearts through faith. And I pray that you, being

rooted and established in love, may have power, together with all the saints, to grasp how wide and long and high and deep is the love of Christ, and to know this love that surpasses knowledge—that you may be filled to the measure of all the fullness of God (Ephesians 3:16-19).

The greatest mystery of all is that we are in Christ—and Christ is in us. As we settle down into the house that God is building, we understand that Christ too is settling down in our hearts. That's what the word *dwell* literally means—that Christ may take up residence, kick off his sandals, and make himself at home.

Paul is already looking ahead to my third point, the *finishing* of the building, which speaks of *being comfortable* in our faith. Pictures and family photos will soon be hung on walls that are being plastered, sanded, and painted. Rough planks are covered up with padding and carpet. Everything is prepared for a long-term occupancy. We move into this house, as Christ moves into our hearts, "through faith" (Ephesians 3:17).

A Time to Tear Down

As Paul alternates between his metaphors—first a building and then a body—he's helping us visualize the spiritual project God is undertaking through Christ. Yes, the church is spiritual, but it's also here and now, the body of believers God has placed us in. Paul toggles back and forth between these two realms, the material and the spiritual, because God too has a foot (so to speak) in both worlds. God is doing something right now that will last for all eternity.

What is the practical application of this to you and me?

In order to grow in faith, we must be intimately connected with God's building project. We must be engaged in the body of believers, the *communio sanctorum*. It's here that we learn to worship, to serve God and others, and to grow into the fullness of Christ. Our faith will grow and be strengthened in practical ways as we live out the corporate design God has for you and me.

Do you remember Asaph? His faltering faith was rekindled when he thought of his connectedness to others, his obligations to the "sanctuary" and to the generation who would follow him (Psalm 73:15-17).

We don't catch faith from others. We don't acquire it through osmosis. We don't believe by proxy. Nevertheless there is a synergistic quality to faith. The story of the four men who carried their paralyzed friend to Christ gives legs to this truth. So far we've focused on what it means to build up, but this story reminds us that there's also a time to tear down and remove obstacles to faith.

> Some men came carrying a paralytic on a mat and tried to take him into the house to lay him before Jesus. When they could not find a way to do this because of the crowd, they went up on the roof and lowered him on his mat through the tiles into the middle of the crowd, right in front of Jesus. When Jesus saw their faith, he said, "Friend, your sins are forgiven" (Luke 5:18-20).

Faith doesn't rub off on us, and we don't get extra credit just for hanging around those who have more faith than we do. But faith does have a collective dimension to it. Jesus heard the noise, saw the debris falling around him, and looked up. What did he see? Luke tells us that "he saw their faith."

We need faithful friends—in every sense of the word. On all four sides of our mat, we need to be surrounded by those who keep faith with us and keep faith with God. We need friends who will tear out a roof in order to build up our faith—friends who will do whatever it takes to lower us into the middle of the room, "right in front of Jesus."

Summing-Up: Our faith is meant to be nurtured and expressed within the church. Believers are bound together in a community of faith; our common confession of faith in Christ forms the basis of our fellowship. We were never meant to be spiritual freelancers but to participate fully in the "communion of saints" that God is building.

For Further Reflection

1. How does the world's definition of community differ from the church's? What should Christians hold in common? What should bind us together?

2. How has the community of believers helped to nurture your faith? Are there specific examples you can cite?

3. Has your faith ever been hindered by the community of believers? How did you handle this?

4. Who are the faithful friends in your life who would carry you to Jesus? Are you this kind of friend to others?

CHAPTER 12

Simplified by Faith

Key Idea: **Faith cuts through the clutter of failure to simplify our lives before God and others.**

I'M TRYING TO BELIEVE, BUT I JUST CAN'T."

For many people, the challenge of faith is like trying to lay an egg. *They just can't do it.* Faith seems to place impossible demands on the mind, will, and emotions. If only there were a switch we could activate—an "on button" that we could push. Then faith would be easy.

Sometimes too we think it must have been a simpler task "back then" to believe. Certainly, the men and women of the Bible had an easier time of it (we think), since God spoke to them, appeared to them, and performed amazing feats of power that validated his presence. By comparison, faith seems complicated and difficult to us.

But faith never complicates life. It only simplifies. It simplifies the choices that lie before us—the "how do I live my life" kind of questions that we'll never stop facing. But it simplifies us too as we look back at the twists and turns of our lives, and as others look back at us and remember what our lives amounted to. Faith cuts through the clutter of competing alternatives. Faith blazes a trail through the thicket of doubt, confusion, and everyday experience with the clarity of a single big idea: *God can be trusted, and that's why living by faith is always worth it in the end.*

These truths were inscribed into the lives of the great faith models of the

169

Old Testament. In this chapter, we'll look at five of them—Noah, Abraham, Moses, David, and Elijah. These men were pathfinders in the journey of faith. They went ahead of us, blazing the trail, so that we can follow in their steps.

> *Faith is the simple, unswerving conviction that God is good, that he desires good things for us, and that we can trust him to be faithful right to the end.*

How can we believe? We start believing when we stop trying so hard and start following the path that others have already cut through the wilderness. As we do this, as we hitch our wagon to the train ahead of us, we begin to see that faith is turning our back on something and leaving it behind. Faith is also turning toward something, no matter how far off it might be. And faith is plodding along right now, not giving up, through all the mountain passes and river crossings that lie ahead.

That's it. Faith is renunciation, hope, and obedience. It's the simple, unswerving conviction that God is good, that he desires good things for us, and that we can trust him to be faithful right to the end.

One of my most memorable vacations was the several days spent with my wife and two children at a dude ranch high in the mountains of Wyoming. If I were still in the fourth grade, this would be my topic for "What I Did Last Summer." I'd describe how the Pinnacle Buttes rise up sharply around the old hunting lodge. I'd describe the rough-hewn logs and the great stone fireplace and the black-and-white photographs of cowboys from the 1920s.

I'd describe the horseback riding and how our little group entered the meadow at the crest of a hill and looked far down into the valley. A mile or so ahead we could see the other team that had left the lodge some time before. They were slowly working their way home ahead of us.

Now think again of faith. Look off in the distance, down the valley, through the open field, by the winding river. You can see the pack ahead of us. They're pretty far down the trail—too far to catch up to. But we can see them, and we can follow them. And even when they disappear for a while into a grove of trees or around a bend, we can still follow, because there's a path before us.

Hurry up. Let's join them. It's a beautiful journey.

Finding Grace

If you were a peasant living in fourteenth-century England, you would have known something about Noah. But you would have known more about his wife. You would be illiterate, of course, so what you knew about the Bible was pretty much limited to what you saw etched into stained-glass windows or reenacted in pageant plays each year in the town square.

These dramas simplified the stories of the Bible in all the wrong ways. Noah's wife is not even named in Scripture, but she snagged the lead role in medieval reenactments, the part that every actor would kill for. She's a nag and a shrew, and she has no intention of getting on board "that thing" sitting in the front yard. She doesn't want to leave her friends behind. And so Noah has to drag her kicking and screaming onto the ark. The compelling, biblical portrait of a man of faith was thereby reduced to a Punch and Judy routine played out for comic effect.

God simplified Noah's life a little differently. "But Noah found grace in the eyes of the LORD" (Genesis 6:8 NKJV). In a world that was unspeakably corrupt, Noah "walked with God" (Genesis 6:9).

Like that medieval peasant, you and I have become fairly comfortable with Noah. He's a stock figure in the storybook Bibles we read to our children. But do we really know him? Do we have any earthly idea what it meant for Noah to walk with God? The prophet Amos asked, "Can two walk together unless they have agreed to do so?" (Amos 3:3) To walk with God means to be in step with him and out of step with the world.

Consider this. Faith for Noah meant accepting a whole set of propositions that must have seemed counterintuitive and counterfactual. It meant rejecting what all the best climate experts, all the talking heads, all the PhDs had to say. It meant the most complete rejection of this world ever documented in human history. It meant looking ahead to another world that Noah could not even begin to imagine. At some point in his long life, Noah made the decision to follow God instead of the world. And then he persisted in that obedience for many years.

The Bible tells us more. It tells us that Noah got off the ark and fell off the wagon. He lapsed into drunkenness after he harvested the first crop of grapes in the new world (Genesis 9:20-21). But you'll read none of that in the New Testament. As we look back at him, we're left with God's assessment: Noah found grace, he found favor, in the eyes of the Lord. And this is how his life was simplified by faith.

You might be saying, "That's a great Sunday school lesson, but I just can't believe the story itself. I can't believe it really happened—that there was this flood, and that a man named Noah built an ark and took all these animals with him. It sounds like a fairy tale!"

> *Don't let your questions become an excuse to ignore the voice of God.*

I'm not going to tell you about fossils on mountains or flood stories among Native Americans. I'm not going to tell you any of this because skeptics have their answers to every piece of evidence I might give. Not to mention, all the argumentation would only get in the way of what God is saying to us. I don't want to do that. I don't want to interrupt God's story.

Here's what I suggest instead. Don't ignore your questions or your doubts. But don't try to settle the "facts" of the matter either. Instead, focus first on what's really important and let God start with that. Most importantly, don't let your questions become an excuse to ignore the voice of God. Look at Noah's life with eyes of faith. Hear the story with your heart, and then live accordingly. God will do the rest. He will simplify your questions just as he wants to simplify your life.

The Friend of God

If you want to live by faith, then you need to follow Abraham. That's the message of both the Old and New Testaments. Abraham is so closely connected with the life of faith that his name is almost shorthand for faith itself. He's the gold standard, the prototype. I'm tempted to say that God broke the mold when he made Abraham—but that would be misleading. Abraham *is* the mold that God wants to press us into.

The apostle Paul designates Abraham as "the father of all who believe" (Romans 4:11). He is thus the greatest faith example in Scripture. Paul refers us to Abraham when he lays out the doctrine of justification: "The righteous will live by faith" (Galatians 3:11). In every sense, then—from the daily, practical experience of faith to the loftiest expression of theology—Abraham is our reference point.

How does Abraham illustrate the life of faith? In three important ways:

- what he's called from
- what he's called to
- how he gets from the one place to the other

We see the principles of renunciation, hope, and obedience at every stage of his life.

When we first encounter him, he's called Abram, and he's a passing reference at the end of a genealogical list: "Terah took his son Abram, his grandson Lot son of Haran, and his daughter-in-law Sarai, the wife of his son Abram, and together they set out from Ur of the Chaldeans to go to Canaan. But when they came to Haran, they settled there" (Genesis 11:31).

What we know is incomplete and fragmentary, the way family histories always are. Abram is already in Haran, north of Canaan, when he first comes into focus. He arrived there as part of an extended family, led by his father Terah. Genesis 12 will tell us that God spoke to Abram when he was in Haran and told him to move out toward Canaan. But when Stephen gave his great sermon before Israel's religious leaders, he said that God spoke to Abram when he was in Mesopotamia: "'Brothers and fathers, listen to me! The God of glory appeared to our father Abraham while he was still in Mesopotamia, before he lived in Haran'" (Acts 7:2).

So which is it? When did God speak to Abram?

We don't know the full sequence here. We have a lot of questions, as always. If I were writing Abraham's biography as a modern historian, I would want answers to these questions. But Scripture doesn't give us a clear chronology. We don't have anything approaching what a modern historian demands—a rigorously detailed time line, cross-checked with documentary evidence that plots Abraham's journey. But there are no real, or necessary, contradictions here. The life of Abraham is a spiritual biography. We can be sure that at some point God began to speak to Abraham, somehow, someway, in some place. Scripture is describing a process of spiritual growth—the awakening of faith in Abraham's life. God spoke to him in Haran just as he had been speaking to him in Mesopotamia.

Growing up in Sunday school, where all the saints of the Bible were made out of flannelgraph, I always assumed that when the Bible says, "And God spoke," that God, in fact, *spoke*—verbally, audibly, in a deep reverberating voice.

We know that God did speak that way sometimes. Little Samuel heard God call his name in the middle of the night (1 Samuel 3:1-14). But was this typical?

Perhaps Abraham sensed the moving of God in his heart. Perhaps he looked around and was disgusted at the idolatry, materialism, and immorality of the sophisticated Mesopotamians. That was God moving upon his heart, pulling him away from this world to the things of God. Don't we also describe God speaking to us that way in the still, small movements of our heart?

> *Faith advances on the heels of a rejection—a rejection of the false promises of this world.*

We know quite a bit about the world that Abram's family left behind. Mesopotamia was already an ancient civilization by the time Abram was born, somewhere in the Fertile Crescent in a place the Bible identifies only as Ur of the Chaldees. In the nineteenth century, when archaeologists first began to excavate the mound cities near the Tigris and Euphrates Rivers, the sensational claims could be read in newspapers on both sides of the Atlantic: *Abraham's Home Discovered!*

A lot of newspapers were sold, but there was little truth in the headlines. Abraham did come from Mesopotamia, but from a much later period than the culture being revealed by the archaeologists' spades. Still, the discoveries were enormously important in shaping our understanding of the biblical world. As archaeologists turned their spades and studied what they found, a sophisticated and advanced civilization began to emerge. This is what Abraham left behind.

Abraham was called out from an idolatrous, materialistic culture—a culture much like our own. He was called to reject that, to turn his back on it, to renounce its hold over his life. Faith advances on the heels of a rejection—a rejection of the false promises of this world.

Hundreds of years later, when Israel had finally grasped the long-awaited promise and entered the land, Joshua looked back and put everything in its proper spiritual perspective: "Long ago your forefathers, including Terah the father of Abraham and Nahor, lived beyond the River and worshiped other gods" (Joshua 24:2).

This is one of the ways that Abraham is a paradigm for us. He's the model for faith. Every act of faith is a turning away from idols. In what sense? When I walk by sight, I'm substituting the things of this world for the promises of God. Every spiritual lesson that Abraham learned was codified into law at Mount Sinai. Walking by faith is a very specific way to fulfill the First Commandment—having no other gods before the one true God.

He was called to a new place—the "promised land," the place of God's blessing. As the writer of Hebrews puts it, "He went out, not knowing where he was going" (11:8 ESV). He "was looking forward to the city with foundations, whose architect and builder is God" (11:10). He fixed his spiritual eyes upon a destination, just as the apostle Paul was reaching for the "prize of the high calling of God in Christ Jesus" (Philippians 3:14 KJV).

But to get there, he had to journey like a pilgrim, and moving from one place to another is always a hassle. He had to deal with petty chieftains and persistent squabbling over land rights. He had to bail out a dysfunctional family member, his nephew Lot. He had servants to train, wells to dig, enemies to placate. None of this was very tidy. None of it was pretty.

Abraham wasn't always focused and consistent. Sometimes his attention drifted. He seemed to waver in his faith sometimes. How else can we describe his detour into Egypt (Genesis 12:10-20) or his attempt to produce an heir with Hagar (Genesis 16)?

That's how the story reads in Genesis. But when we turn to the New Testament, we seem to be reading about somebody entirely different: "Yet he did not waver through unbelief regarding the promise of God, but was strengthened in his faith and gave glory to God, being fully persuaded that God had power to do what he had promised" (Romans 4:20-21).

That doesn't sound like the Abraham who pitches his tent across the pages of Genesis. In the New Testament we read about a man who's been simplified by faith. We read about a man who's remembered as the "friend of God" (James 2:23). We see Abraham as God sees him, with his faith brought to completion by grace.

Between what we leave behind and the hope that lies before us, there is always a journey—the day-by-day experience of obedience to God. It's common today to hear the Christian life described as a journey. There's some truth in this, but also a lot of Zen-like nonsense. The journey is important, but the Christian life is much more than way stations and scenic overpasses.

The journey of faith gains meaning only in light of what we've left behind and where we're going. A journey can exist only from point A to point B—from, say, Poughkeepsie, New York, to Walla Walla, Washington. If we emphasize the journey by itself, without recognizing that it occurs *from* one place *to* another, then we're missing an important dimension of the Christian life—its renunciation of one world and acceptance by faith of another. All the stuff between Poughkeepsie and Walla Walla gets sloughed off in time. All that I'm struggling with now—my doubts, my failures—everything will be simplified in God's final estimation of my life.

> *All that I'm struggling with now—my doubts, my failures—everything will be simplified in God's final estimation of my life.*

Baskets and Burning Bushes

Here's my problem when I turn to the life of Moses. I've never encountered God in a burning bush. I've never stood on a mountain that's wrapped in the fingers of God's glory. The Creator of the universe has never called me by name. Not literally. Not audibly. What exactly can Moses teach *me* about the life of faith? Isn't Moses just another one of those unique Bible figures, like Abraham, whose life is never to be duplicated or imitated?

The life of Moses is marked by spectacular changes in scenery—from the bulrushes of the Nile to Pharaoh's court, to the desert and then back to Pharaoh's court, and ultimately, to Mount Sinai and the glory of God. And that's just the highlights reel. There are three great turning points in his life, when things could have gone very differently.

From the moment he was born, everything about Moses seemed extraordinary. His parents certainly saw this, since they went to great lengths to protect their baby son from Pharaoh's henchmen. Exodus gives us the story line, but Hebrews 11 draws out the theology behind what happened: "By faith Moses' parents hid him for three months after he was born, because they saw he was no ordinary child, and they were not afraid of the king's edict" (Hebrews 11:23).

They saw he was no ordinary child. Moses' rescue from certain death was extraordinary. Pharaoh's daughter just happened to appear along the banks of the Nile, heard his cry, and took pity on the infant. This was the first great turning point of Moses's life.

Perhaps his birth and rescue are too extraordinary for the modern mind. I remember how a family member of mine began her journey toward unbelief in these very bulrushes along the Nile. She read somewhere that the birth story of Moses was copied from the birth story of Sargon the Great, the Akkadian potentate who ruled Mesopotamia in the third millennium BC. Never mind that the story of Sargon was written down so late that it was just as likely copied from the story of Moses. That possibility never seems to occur to the skeptics.

It all must have seemed pretty incredible to Moses too. He had been plucked from the Nile by Pharaoh's daughter, and he grew up in the king's court. His formative years were spent in luxury and privilege. We know this much from Exodus, the second book of the Bible.

But when we turn to the New Testament, we gain another perspective. Faith cuts through the thicket and complexity of Pharaoh's court with a single, unavoidable decision. *Whom will I follow? How will I live? What direction will I go?* Faith required renunciation of all the privilege. Moses, no less than Abraham, had to turn his back on the materialism of this world if he was ever to see the glory of God.

> By faith Moses, when he had grown up, refused to be known as the son of Pharaoh's daughter. He chose to be mistreated along with the people of God rather than to enjoy the pleasures of sin for a short time. He regarded disgrace for the sake of Christ as of greater value than the treasures of Egypt, because he was looking ahead to his reward (Hebrews 11:24-26).

This was the second great turning point of Moses's life—and he didn't navigate through this moment altogether well. He killed a man. Exodus tells us that Moses saw the suffering of his people, the Hebrews, and he struck down an abusive Egyptian. Moses was now cut off from the life of privilege. He lifted his hand in anger and became a revolutionary. He made his decision and then executed it with violent force. He wasn't ready to be used fully by God. His self-will had to be dealt with. Still, apathy and indifference would have been the far worse response.

Moses fled for his life into the desert where he lived in simple anonymity for 40 years. We can forget how ordinary much of Moses's life really was. There were vast stretches when nothing much happened, when he saw nothing lying before him but the unchanging landscape of the desert. But then, out of all the sameness and routine, a bush burst into flames, and he heard the voice of God (Exodus 3:1-6). He returned to Egypt and led God's people toward the land of promise.

> All the failures and shortcomings of Moses are swept aside by one simple fact: He served God.

How is Moses remembered? How was he simplified by faith? God, who is the ultimate master of simplification, initiates the process. He announced to Joshua that "Moses *my servant* is dead" (Joshua 1:2, emphasis added). This phrase, "the servant of the Lord," would become the divine simplification of Moses's life, right through the end of the Old Testament (Malachi 4:4) and the end of the New (Revelation 15:3).

More than anything, we remember the obedience of Moses. Hebrews tells us that he "was faithful as a servant in all God's house, testifying to what would be said in the future" (Hebrews 3:5). Once again, all the failures and shortcomings of this man are swept aside by one simple fact: *He served God.*

Head-Hunting Strategies

David, the shepherd-king and "sweet psalmist" of Israel (2 Samuel 23:1), was simplified right from the start. When the first king of Israel, Saul, was careening toward ruin, God told the prophet Samuel that he would give the throne to someone else, "a man after God's own heart" (1 Samuel 13:14). God divulged a big secret to Samuel that day—a secret about how he recruits his servants. We learn from the story of David that God is not a headhunter at all. He's a *heart*-hunter.

We read in 1 Samuel 16 that God directed Samuel to the little town of Bethlehem and the house of Jesse. One by one the sons of Jesse were brought before the prophet; and one by one God rejected them. "Are there any more sons?" Samuel asked. Jesse must have hemmed and hawed. We can hear the reluctance in his voice, even in translation. Jesse tells the prophet that there was one more son, though he couldn't possibly be the one Samuel was look-ing for. He was out tending the flock. There was little potential in him.

Little potential? God had already seen David's heart—and that's what God would always see, from beginning to end. God saw his heart when the ruddy-faced shepherd trotted in from the field, and he saw it years later when the royal house was in shambles. The story would become sordid and tragic. David would become enslaved to lust and envy and end up killing a man so he could take his wife, Bathsheba. Despite his enormous failures, despite all the detours and disappointments of his later life, David's heart still thirsted for the living God (Psalm 42:1). That's how God simplified him.

God never canceled out that first assessment, because it's a faith descrip-tion—it's what God sees, what God *always saw*, when he looked at David. Paul picked up the phrase, first found in Habakkuk, that "the just shall live by faith." Paul was the great apostle of God's grace, and he understood that God does not see us through the filter of what we've done or how we've lived. God sees us through the righteousness of Jesus Christ. God looks at me and he doesn't see my many failures. Because of faith—because of my commit-ment to the promises of God—he sees me as righteous. He *simplifies* my life. And the most profound simplification of my life is that I am *in Christ*.

The Prophet from Nowhere

Elijah is an enigma, a flesh-and-blood mystery. He appears out of nowhere, flashing across the pages of Scripture like a meteorite. And he leaves the same way—in a flaming chariot. One moment he's eyeball-to-eyeball with King Ahab and Queen Jezebel. The next he's running for his life. He was a walking contradiction. What made him tick?

We don't have much to go on since the Bible is notoriously sparse with biographical details. Characters just drop onto the page with virtually no backstory. They wander onto the movie set, blinking beneath the lights. Somebody hands them a script and says, "Start reading." They never went to kindergarten, never had a first date, never learned to ride a bike. They just appear, fully formed, slightly dazed with God's call still ringing in their ears.

Elijah's entry on stage is like this. He appears in 1 Kings 17:1 with nothing more than an obscure, passing reference to his background: "Now Elijah the Tishbite, from Tishbe in Gilead, said to Ahab, 'As the LORD lives, whom I serve, there will be neither dew nor rain in the next few years except at my word.'"

From Tishbe in Gilead. That's it. That's all we know about him. No formal introduction at all. We're not even sure where Tishbe is. Elijah simply materializes before one of Israel's worst kings and tells him to get ready for the drought of the century. At this point we know nothing of his qualifications to make such a claim. Presumably, King Ahab knew a little more than we do or this strange, bombastic man from the sticks never would have gained access to the throne.

We don't write biographies this way. We want to know where somebody came from; we want to know all the little details that made the man. Where did Elijah's boldness come from? Why was he given to fits of despair? Who influenced him during his formative years? Was he ever disappointed in love?

But none of these things matter when it comes to faith. Elijah's shortcomings don't matter all that much either—his depression, self-pity, paranoia, and panic attacks. We look back at Elijah from the vantage point of the New Testament, and we see something different: "Elijah was a man just like us. He prayed earnestly that it would not rain, and it did not rain on the land for three and a half years" (James 5:17).

We see his boldness in the face of evil and his confidence in the power of God. In other words, we see what God sees.

Simplify Me, When I'm Dead

Keith Douglas, one of the most talented British poets of World War II, left a slim body of work when he was killed in action in North Africa. He was 24. His lyrical, detached observations on war have seldom been matched in intensity. One poem in particular reads as his personal elegy. In "Simplify Me, When I'm Dead," Douglas imagines what his life, what his bones, will turn to with the passage of time. Archaeologists will pick over his chalky remains and simplify him with a label. The poet has one request, which book-ends the poem like a refrain:

> *Remember me when I am dead*
> *and simplify me when I'm dead.*

That's how I feel, but not in some morbid sense. I too want my life to be simplified. God created me out of nothing, and I have no potential in myself to be anything but a short-term dweller in tents. Of my bones, nothing spectacular will ever be said. But God has given me the chance to migrate beyond my own boundaries. I have hope beyond myself—and this is the essence of faith.

Michelangelo said that "faith in oneself is the best and safest course." But that's just not true. Faith in oneself is a miserable dead end. Lot had faith in himself, and he ended up in Sodom, a city with no future. His uncle Abraham was looking for a city whose builder and maker is God. That's the choice for me. I want to outlast myself, outlive my "self," and Abraham gives me hope that I will do that.

> *I have hope beyond myself—and this is the essence of faith.*

Like Abraham and every other hero of faith, I want my whole life to be summed up by a single great decision to follow God. That's the moment when I stumbled onto the movie set. That's when a script was thrust into my hands, and I heard a voice from the director's chair say, "Don't worry, I'll coach you through it. You'll be great!"

That's how faith simplifies us.

I think of how my Great-Grandfather Wilkins lived on as a memory in my family. I never knew him. He exists to me only as a black-and-white patriarch in a single brittle photograph. I see him bearded and austere, sitting like Father Abraham in a yard somewhere in early twentieth-century Kansas. All around him are his kinfolk, as they used to be called—family as innumerable as the sands of the sea.

That's all I know about him—this old photograph and that he never tasted ice cream in his entire life. At least that's the story I was told. He refused to try ice cream because he didn't like it—even though he'd never tried it. Not once. A century or so after his death, this odd scrap of memory is the simplification of his life. The cruel economy of time always does that, always reduces us to a mere sentence. How will my sentence read?

Faith causes me to look beyond my mortality. It leads me to contemplate how the world without me will be different because of the choices I've made. What will the landscape look like once the pegs of my tent are pulled up? Will anything be left of me after the sheep and goats of my life have all been distributed? Fifty or a hundred years from now, someone may mention me in a passing conversation. What will they say?

I hope my life is simplified in all the right ways.

He was a man who loved God.
He was faithful to his wife, and he raised his children well.
He knew where he was going, and, unlike his great-grandfather, he enjoyed a little ice cream along the way.

I hope they say something like that.

Summing-Up: The great heroes of the Bible show us that God views us through the filter of our faith. Despite our shortcomings and failures, God always sees the heart that trusts him. Our lives should be simplified by faith—reduced to a single great choice to renounce the world's false promises and press faithfully toward all that God has planned for us.

For Further Reflection

1. Why can it be hard to identify with the faith heroes of the Bible? In many ways, their experiences were different from ours. In what ways were they like us?

2. What does following Christ require you to renounce? Be specific as you look at your life and the society that you're a part of.

3. What is accurate and what is misleading about describing the Christian life as a journey? How is this metaphor sometimes misused?

4. Imagine that a hundred years from now somebody mentions you in a conversation. What do you want them to say about you? If your life could be reduced to one sentence, what would it be?

CHAPTER 13

A Cloud of Witnesses

Key Idea: We are spurred on to
faith by the examples of believers
who have gone before us.

WE'RE BEING WATCHED. Whether we like it or not, cameras are focused on us from every angle. In London, for example, over a half million surveillance cameras are posted throughout the city—on the corners of buildings, on buses, in the Underground, and at intersections. The average Londoner can expect to be videotaped some 300 times in an ordinary day, and this is increasingly true of most large Western cities. It would seem that George Orwell's nightmare vision of Big Brother is coming true.

We're being watched from above too. Type your home address into Google Earth, and you can view your property from outer space. You can also get a street-level view, if you'd like. The picture of my property was taken during the summer, judging from the sprinkler pattern I detect on the driveway. There's no sign of life in the windows, but I do see a little black shadow at the edge of the porch. That's my dog, Scruffy—in very low resolution. He's standing at the edge of the steps, barking at the Google Maps Camera Car that must have been driving by very slowly.

The human mind is hard at work figuring out how to track me and use that information to someone else's financial advantage. Radio tracking devices are now embedded in credit cards; some are even sewn into designer clothing. Nearly everything we buy may someday be traceable. The frequency from these little devices generally broadcasts a few feet and no farther, but if radio receivers become as common as surveillance cameras, then it's easy to imagine how our every move might be tracked by the credit card in our pocket or the shirt on our back.

I'm being watched—and I don't find that very comforting.

Heavenly Spectators

But I'm also being watched from heaven. Not just by satellites that can read license plate numbers. Not by malevolent alien beings plotting to invade earth. I'm being watched by every saint who has ever lived: "Therefore, since we are surrounded by such a great cloud of witnesses, let us throw off everything that hinders and the sin that so easily entangles, and let us run with perseverance the race marked out for us" (Hebrews 12:1).

The word for "cloud" in the original Greek, *nephos*, can be used both in a literal and metaphorical sense. It's how you describe an actual cloud in the sky; but it's also a poetic way of saying "an innumerable throng, a multitude."

I like how most English translations keep the metaphor, *cloud,* instead of turning it into something more prosaic, like *crowd,* which is technically what it refers to. With clouds come echoes of the glory of God. The saints in heaven are a glorious throng. They're like spectators in a cosmic sports arena—not the drunk, rowdy kind at a soccer match in Manchester. These heavenly spectators, clothed in white, are intoxicated with God's glory as they cheer us toward the finish line.

The writer of Hebrews clearly wants us to view this cloud as a divinely appointed resource in our walk of faith. That's why he mentioned them as a postscript to his long list of heroes—those patriarchs and prophets of Hebrews 11. But how do they help us? They are *there,* after all, and we are *here.* What can they really do for us?

We learn from their lives, but only if we remember their stories. "These things happened to them as examples," Paul wrote, "and were written down as warnings for us, on whom the fulfillment of the ages has come" (1 Corinthians 10:11). In another letter Paul writes that "everything that was written in the past was written to teach us, so that through endurance and the encouragement of the Scriptures we might have hope" (Romans 15:4). We need all the help—and all the hope—we can get.

Believers have a rich and noble pedigree. This is our identity. It's who we are—"a chosen people, a royal priesthood, a holy nation, a people belonging to God" (1 Peter 2:9). We shouldn't take our family for granted or forget their history. We shouldn't let these godly lights fade into oblivion because we're too busy trying to reinvent the church and make it relevant.

Is it any wonder that so many Christians struggle with doubt when we don't even know who we are? The believer who doubts is suffering an identity crisis. He's forgotten what family he belongs to. He's lost track of his brothers and sisters.

> *The believer who doubts is suffering an identity crisis. He's forgotten what family he belongs to.*

Things were very different in the early church. They kept alive the memory of the saints. The cloud of witnesses spurred them on with faith and hope, and we would do well to learn from their example.

Who Was Rufus?

We see the cloud forming very early in the church—as early as the pages of the New Testament. In the Gospel of Mark, for example, we read of a man named Simon of Cyrene who was compelled to carry Christ's cross: "A certain man from Cyrene, Simon, the father of Alexander and Rufus, was passing by on his way in from the country, and they forced him to carry the cross" (Mark 15:21).

Matthew and Luke relate this incident as well, but Mark is alone in adding the family details. Why does Mark tell us that Simon was "the father of Alexander and Rufus"? Most of the characters in the Gospel narratives are not identified like this, so what makes him special? Alexander and Rufus were probably known in the church, and this is Mark's way of personalizing the story of the crucifixion.

We find a clue, perhaps, when we turn to the final chapter of Romans. Paul is greeting the believers who were well-known to him from the Roman church: "Greet Rufus, chosen in the Lord, and his mother, who has been a mother to me too" (Romans 16:13). We can't be certain—names being what they are—but it's a real possibility that this is the same man Mark identified as Simon's son. Mark probably wrote his Gospel from the Christian community in Rome, the very church Paul is addressing and the very church where Rufus was a well-known member.

The old Negro spiritual asks, "Were you there when they crucified my

Lord?" Simon the Cyrenian could have responded, "Yes, I was there. I carried the cross. I saw the quiet suffering of the Lord and I believed." Long after his death, Simon's sons would have testified to another generation of believers. We can imagine how people would have pointed out Rufus in the Roman church. "That's Rufus. His father was Simon, the one who carried the cross of our Lord." And that's why we know about Simon, because he's part of the great cloud of witnesses.

> *We look beyond what's here and now, whether we understand all the details or not, and we trust what God is doing.*

The cloud was already forming before Jesus died. Simon shows us that. But so does the woman who broke open an alabaster box to anoint the Lord. Jesus was in Bethany; he was on his way to Jerusalem for the last time. A woman brought a jar of precious perfume, broke the jar, and poured the perfume on his head. The disciples were indignant at the waste of so much money that could have been given to the poor. Jesus responded by identifying their hypocrisy ("'The poor you will always have with you'") and then praising the woman for what she did.

> "She did what she could. She poured perfume on my body beforehand to prepare for my burial. I tell you the truth, wherever the gospel is preached throughout the world, what she has done will also be told, in memory of her" (Mark 14:8-9).

The pure essence of our faith is like this perfume, an aroma that pleases God. "She did what she could"—that's what faith is. We look beyond what's here and now, whether we understand all the details or not, and we trust what God is doing. This woman has taken her place among the cloud of witnesses cheering us on in every small act of faith.

We can go back further, into the ministry of Jesus, for another early member of the cloud. When Jesus entered Jerusalem, a blind man named Bartimaeus called out to him: "'Jesus, Son of David, have mercy on me!'" (Mark 10:47). Why is he named in the story? And why is his father identified (Bartimaeus means "son of Timaeus")? Most of the miracle stories don't give us these details. The probable explanation, once again, is that Bartimaeus was well-known in the early church. He had a unique testimony—Jesus healed him! When he opened his eyes, the first person he saw was Jesus.

The early church kept these stories of faith alive in the oral accounts that circulated among the first generation of believers. Eventually, they were written down in the Gospels and transferred to you and me. These New Testament heroes of faith, like the Old Testament saints listed in Hebrews 11, are watching us with great interest. They were there before us, they know the path, and we should follow them.

An Exclusive Club

Groucho Marx said, "I don't want to belong to any club that will accept me as a member." I can't imagine ever saying that about the church, since it's not a club and I really am glad to belong to it. But I understand what Groucho meant. *Accept me as a member? Who am I?*

Paul felt that way. He called himself "the least of the apostles" (1 Corinthians 15:9) and the worst of sinners (1 Timothy 1:15). That's what my attitude should truly be—a sense of unworthiness to be a part of God's great project that spans the ages.

Nothing makes me feel more unworthy than to think of those in the cloud of witnesses who have died for their faith. Martyrdom is a remote abstraction to me as a western Christian. I'm used to comfort and leisure. I'm used to Christianity on my terms. But martyrdom was a living, and a dying, reality for the early believers. Even now Christians throughout the world balance each day on the sharp edge of persecution and death.

We honor these saints with the term *martyr.* The word derives from *martus* in the Greek, and it simply meant "witness." This is how it's translated in Acts 1:8, where Jesus is speaking to his disciples: "'But you will receive power when the Holy Spirit comes on you; and you will be my witnesses in Jerusalem, and in all Judea and Samaria, and to the ends of the earth.'"

"You will be my *martus.*" The word was used to describe a witness in court. Specifically, the disciples were to be witnesses to the resurrection, giving first-person testimony that Christ is alive (Acts 2:32, 3:15, 4:33). We too have been called before the courtroom of the world to bear witness to Christ, to testify that "Christ lives in me" (Galatians 2:20).

Believers of every age, in both the Old and New Testaments, have been called to testify that God is alive and active in the world. This was God's ultimate purpose for his people Israel; it's why he called them out from the nations. Isaiah evokes the imagery of a courtroom as he delivers this message from God.

> All the nations gather together
> and the peoples assemble.
> Which of them foretold this
> and proclaimed to us the former things?
> Let them bring in their witnesses to prove they were right,
> so that others may hear and say, "It is true."
> "*You are my witnesses*," declares the LORD,
> "and my servant whom I have chosen,
> so that you may know and believe me
> and understand that I am he.
> Before me no god was formed,
> nor will there be one after me.
> I, even I, am the LORD,
> and apart from me there is no savior.
> I have revealed and saved and proclaimed—
> I, and not some foreign god among you.
> *You are my witnesses*," declares the LORD, "that I am God."
> (Isaiah 43:9-12, emphasis added)

In the Septuagint, the Greek translation of the Old Testament produced about 200 years before Christ, *martus* was the word used in this passage for "witness."

Right from the beginning of the church, however, *martyr* seems to have been acquiring its specialized meaning. Stephen stood before his accusers as though in a court of law (Acts 7). He delivered his testimony—a masterful exposition of the Old Testament prophecies about Christ. Stephen was stoned to death for his witness, and he became the first martyr in the new, Christian sense of the word. He sealed his testimony with his own blood; he gave witness by laying down his life.

Early in church history martyrs were specially honored. There were plenty of them during the Roman centuries, and many died during intense waves of persecution. The names of many martyrs are still well-known—more so in the Catholic and Orthodox churches where feast days honor the saints. But

Christians of many denominations have heard of Valentine, Sebastian, and even Perpetua. More than others, the heart-rending story of Perpetua seemed to capture the imagination of early Christians. She died in the Roman city of Carthage, in North Africa, in 203 AD.

Perpetua was a 22-year-old woman of noble birth who had everything, in a worldly sense, to lose. A wife and the mother of a young son, Perpetua was condemned to die in the arena. Her father was a pagan; every day he brought Perpetua's son in his arms and pleaded with her to recant her faith in Christ. While imprisoned and awaiting execution, Perpetua wrote a first-hand account of her ordeal.

"My father," Perpetua said. "You see this pitcher. Can we call it by any other name than what it is?"

"No," he said.

"Nor can I call myself by any other name than that of Christian."

Perpetua was led to the arena to face a boar, a leopard, a bear, and a wild bull. She was part of a group of Christians that included Felicitas, a young woman who was eight months pregnant. The women were attacked by the bull, tossed in the air, and gored. But they didn't die. Finally, a gladiator was ordered to put them to death by sword. The crowds came to see blood; but they saw faith instead.

It's right that we remember the persecuted church, both past and present. For generations, *Foxe's Book of Martyrs* has been a perennial bestseller among Christians. It's pretty ghoulish reading, but it's also inspiring, encouraging, and convicting as we reflect upon the sacrifices that Christians before us were willing to make. The martyrs teach us that "to live is Christ and to die is gain" (Philippians 1:21). It's biblical to remember them. Jesus spoke of the prophets who were killed (Matthew 23:37). Martyrs are mentioned too in the long list of Old Testament saints in Hebrews 11. It's interesting, however, that those who were "sawed in two" (Hebrews 11:37) are given no special commendation above those who, like Jacob, died comfortably in their bed at a very old age.

> *The martyrs teach us that "to live is Christ and to die is gain." It's biblical to remember them.*

With their stories of courage and sacrifice, it's easy to see why martyrdom was soon viewed as an exclusive club within the church. But this led to an unfortunate distortion of the biblical concept of *witness*. In the catacombs beneath Rome, the burial sites of martyrs became hallowed chambers. In the centuries that followed, relics were plundered from their graves and began to appear in churches across the Christian world where they became objects of reverence and even superstition. What was lost in the medieval veneration of saints is the truth that every believer is a saint, and every saint is a martyr, at least in the sense that Jesus meant when he sent his disciples out into the world (Acts 1:8).

Different Ways of Dying

There's more than one way to die, if you're a Christian. Paul speaks of three types of dying that should be true of every believer in every culture. We are to die to ourselves, die to the world, and die to sin. This kind of witness, or martyrdom, comes about only as we identify with Christ through faith.

The most basic kind of martyr, if we can put it in those terms, is the disciple. *Dying to self* is what discipleship is all about. Paul said, "I have been crucified with Christ and I no longer live, but Christ lives in me" (Galatians 2:20). According to Christ's own definition, this is the baseline Christian, the standard issue, the factory model.

> Then Jesus said to his disciples, "If anyone would come after me,
> he must deny himself and take up his cross and follow me. For
> whoever wants to save his life will lose it, but whoever loses his
> life for me will find it" (Matthew 16:24-25).

The disciple is not known for his own identity or his own accomplishments. He's known only for his commitment to follow the Master who called him. In the ultimate expression of self-effacement, the disciple seeks to be conformed to the image of Christ (Romans 8:29). Sometimes he's called to lay down his life, but the disciple is always called to die to himself.

Here's the irony. Even though the disciple is known for self-denial—for losing his life in Christ's—his life should nonetheless stand out as an example for us to follow. Paul said, "Follow my example, as I follow the example of Christ" (1 Corinthians 11:1). Once again, this is how the crowd of witnesses (or martyrs) urges us on toward faith.

Dying to the world is a second form of martyrdom expected of me. It takes faith to live like this—to live as though we truly believe the words of the old gospel song:

This world is not my home,
I'm just a-passing through.
My treasures are laid up
Somewhere beyond the blue.

Paul surrendered all the worldly things that once mattered to him—social position, family pedigree, religious education—and he cast his lot entirely with Christ (Philippians 3:7-8). "May I never boast," Paul said, "except in the cross of our Lord Jesus Christ, through which the world has been crucified to me, and I to the world" (Gala-

> *It requires faith to consider ourselves "dead to sin but alive to God in Christ Jesus."*

tians 6:14). In the end, as he waited for the executioner's blade to come down on his neck, Paul was able to testify that it had all been worth it. He knew that his faith would be fulfilled in the substance of a heavenly reward.

> I have fought the good fight, I have finished the race, I have kept the faith. Now there is in store for me the crown of righteousness, which the Lord, the righteous Judge, will award to me on that day—and not only to me, but also to all who have longed for his appearing (2 Timothy 4:7-8).

Finally, we are to *die to sin*—to mortify the flesh. Again, it requires faith to consider ourselves "dead to sin but alive to God in Christ Jesus" (Romans 6:11). I often feel very alive to sin—alive to anger and jealousy, alive to vanity and selfishness. When sin wells up within me, so do my doubts. *Why do I struggle like this? Why does victory often seem so elusive?*

The life of holiness must be a life of faith, because I'm reaching out beyond every failure and every doubt to the finished person God already sees in me.

Ordinary Sainthood

The cloud of witnesses includes more than martyrs, disciples, pilgrims, and mystics. The cloud is much bigger than that. It includes family members who have gone on before us. It includes all the ordinary saints of the church whether we know their names or not. Let me give you one simple example.

John was a tinker in seventeenth-century England. A tinker was a traveling handyman who worked on metal and repaired objects that were made of tin. One day John was in the town of Bedford, and as he passed through the streets looking for employment, he came upon three or four women sitting in the doorway of a house. They were talking, and John stepped close to hear their conversation. These women—ordinary, uneducated women—were speaking of a new birth. They spoke of how the love of Christ had come into their hearts with forgiveness and deliverance from sin. All this was new and very strange to John, and he listened with great interest.

Many years later, John looked back at this brief encounter in the streets of Bedford and acknowledged that God had used the conversation of these women as one step in the process of bringing him to salvation. John wrote about this in his spiritual autobiography, *Grace Abounding*. But his most famous book, without a doubt, is *The Pilgrim's Progress*. John Bunyan was the tinker who stood in that street in Bedford. And the godly conversation of these women was written into his heart, written into his life, and has continued to bear witness to the generations that followed.

From our perspective, Bunyan is a great member of the cloud of witnesses. But what of those women who sat in the sun and spoke of the incredible grace of God? The church is filled with stories like this, stories of faithfulness in the small things (Luke 16:10)—stories of how God chooses "the foolish things of the world to shame the wise" (1 Corinthians 1:27). I think, for example, of the nearly illiterate but faithful layman who filled the pulpit that day when Charles Spurgeon stumbled in from the snow. He's part of the cloud too.

I can, and I must, learn from the saints who have gone before me. They can help me put everything in perspective, especially when I'm tempted to elevate my struggles above theirs. When my faith is shaken not by persecution but by comfort, then I need to learn from the courage of a young woman who said good-bye to her little boy and faced the wild animals. You see, the great cloud of witnesses does more than encourage me on my way. These men and women of faith are more than my own private cheering section. *They also put me in my place.*

That goes for the countless believers of every age who have witnessed to the truth of the gospel through simple, unspectacular faith. Paul told the early believers, "Make it your ambition to lead a quiet life, to mind your own business and to work with your hands" (1 Thessalonians 4:11). Paul didn't say,

"Make it your ambition to die a spectacular and very public death." These ordinary saints too make up that great cloud of witnesses. We don't know their names—but they too are cheering us on, especially as we navigate by faith through the humdrum of our ordinary lives, punching time cards and packing school lunches for our children. They're shouting in our direction, "Hang in there! It's worth it in the end!"

Once again, we should see the connection between *faith* and *faithfulness*. A life lived out in simple obedience to God is a life "full of faith."

> *A life lived out in simple obedience to God is a life "full of faith."*

Larry's Letter

Which brings me to Larry. The church was full and there were a lot of tears the day we said good-bye to him. Larry was always quick with a joke and even quicker with an encouraging word. I remember him in his Hawaiian shirt, standing at the door of the church and greeting everyone who arrived. He was a leader who most loved being a doorkeeper in the house of the Lord.

At the memorial service we heard Larry speak one more time—in a letter he wrote shortly before dying of cancer. The letter began like this:

> First, let me thank you so much for your prayers and love. I know that your prayers have been for me to be healed. Apparently, the Lord, who knows more than we do, has decided to take me home.
>
> I am sure some of you feel disappointed that your prayers did not avail, but believe me, that is far from true. We all pray for many things, and sometimes God answers yes, sometimes no... but always remember that it is God's choice after all and His will is always best. I know that I am in the best place I could ever want to be, even though I will miss you all.
>
> Please don't be discouraged or give up on prayer. Don't be afraid to tell others of God's love for them. You never know how many lives you might touch. Live a godly example before your family and all those who know you. Don't waste the time God has given you. You will never be sorry that you followed the Lord wholeheartedly because when the end comes, you will be able to

look back with no regret. You will have the peace and joy that passes understanding.

This is the heart of faith—the confidence that we'll never be sorry for following Christ. We'll look back, we'll take in our whole life at a glance, and we'll have no regrets.

Thanks, Larry, for watching my race. Sometimes I feel like the little boy who looks up to see if his mom and dad are in the crowd. Thanks for being there for me. Thanks for your life, for your faith. And thanks for cheering me on right now. I really need it.

Summing-Up: We are encouraged in the life of faith by every believer who has gone before us. Every Christian is called to bear witness to the truth by dying to self, to the world, and to sin. The martyrs of the past encourage us by their great sacrifices. They show us that it's always worth it in the end to be faithful to the one who called us.

For Further Reflection

1. What figures in church history do you draw inspiration from? How are you encouraged by their testimonies?
2. Which type of "martyrdom" (dying to self, to the world, or to sin) do you have the hardest time with?
3. Is your faith encouraged more by the example of famous Christians or by those who are faithful and unknown? Why?
4. Do you have family members or friends who have gone to be with the Lord? In what ways does the memory of their lives strengthen your faith?

CHAPTER 14

The End of the Line

Key Idea: Faith will come to a
perfect end someday when we
see Christ face-to-face.

KEEP YOUR HEADS DOWN," she said, "and walk straight ahead. I'll tell you when to look up."

The tour guide had done this many times before, I'm sure, and she clearly relished this moment—the unveiling of one of nature's greatest wonders.

Both my wife and I had seen the Grand Canyon when we were young. It was a standard stop on the Great American Road Trip, back when families still took trips together. We drove station wagons back then, not minivans, and we stopped for breaks at Stuckey's, not Starbucks. Now Janel and I were sharing the experience, forging a kind of generational link with our own children.

I was curious to see if the canyon had grown smaller, the way houses from one's childhood have a way of doing. Rooms that were once as vast as prairies, hallways that stretched like open highways, and basements that were as remote as China—everything becomes cramped, compacted, and unremarkable when seen as an adult. But what about the canyon?

"You can lift your heads now," she said. And as we did, we took in a scene that was every bit as breathtaking as we remembered. It hadn't shrunk a bit in 35 years.

We posed for pictures before one of nature's greatest backdrops. We peered gingerly over the edge. My children were especially interested in the treasure trove of cameras and sunglasses lying on the ledges below. Our guide then told us that tourists typically spend about 15 minutes staring at the canyon. Once the amazement has worn off, once they have seen the canyon and taken their pictures, they head for the gift shop. According to a survey commissioned by the National Park Service, the average tourist then spends the next 45 minutes or so fingering coffee mugs and coasters, sorting through T-shirts and hoodies, and trying on Native American jewelry.

As we near the end of this book, I'm guessing that you still have doubts. That's why we're not done standing by the rim of the canyon, so to speak. Before we turn away and go to the gift shop, we need to be reminded that a vast landscape stretches out before us. We'll never stop asking questions; and we should never stop searching for answers. But the huge gaps in our knowledge will never be fully spanned. They can't be—they won't be—or God could not be God.

Mind the Gap

Gaps make me think of the London Underground. Ever since 1969, commuters on the Tube have been warned to "mind the gap." The space between the train and the platform is a safety hazard for those who aren't paying attention.

When it comes to faith, we need to mind the gap as well. This is one of the ways we believe.

The phrase "God of the gaps" has been used disparagingly to describe a shrinking deity as imagined by the modern secular world—a God who is increasingly consigned to narrower gaps in human knowledge. The idea goes something like this: *How small God must be—so small that he will have no place to dwell once we've explained away his last hiding places, the last mysterious breaches in human knowledge, the blank pages in our textbooks.* As science advances its naturalistic explanations, there will be less and less room for "superstition" and belief in God. Those of us who still believe will cling to those shrinking gaps and say, "That's where God is! He's in this dark little crack right here!"

But a quiet revolution has been underway for several decades—an intellectual revolution that has seriously shaken the modern certainty that we'll someday unravel all of life's mysteries. In many ways, the gaps are looking bigger again. The mysteries are deeper; the chasms in our understanding are wider. This is good news for the believer who struggles with intellectual doubt—who wonders if his God is big enough to handle even the most audacious claims of science.

There's no disputing that science has unlocked many of the mysteries of matter, right down to the

Our restless minds can settle down into the infinity of God and take comfort in everything we don't understand.

subatomic level. But what about the enormous gap between nothing and something? Where did matter come from in the first place, and why is it so orderly and structured? Science too has unlocked many of the mysteries of life, cracking open the genetic code and mapping out its intricacies. But the gap between organic and inorganic remains. Where did life come from? How do we account for its complexity? Science has also penetrated the mysteries of human consciousness and explored the deepest regions of the brain. But the greatest mystery of the human mind, the nature of consciousness, remains. How does self-awareness emerge from the chemical reactions within brain cells? Why can we think and speak about ourselves?

There are good reasons to believe that these gaps are unbridgeable chasms between the finite and infinite, despite the blustering claims of the world's loudest atheists. The gaps are infinite, and the last time anybody checked, infinity holds enough elbow room even for God.

The so-called "God of the gaps" is not shrinking; he's getting a whole lot bigger the more our knowledge grows. Again, this is good news for the believer who struggles with doubt. Our restless minds can settle down into the infinity of God and take comfort, as Job did, in everything we don't understand.

> Indeed these are the mere edges of His ways,
> And how small a whisper we hear of Him!
> But the thunder of His power who can understand?
> (Job 26:14 NKJV)

Job doesn't imagine a canyon here, though if he'd ever had the chance to visit Arizona on vacation, he might have changed his metaphor. Instead, he imagines us standing at the shoreline of God's glory. We see the waves rippling in and glittering in the sun. Beyond us lies a vast ocean. We know this, but we can't take it all in. It's simply too much for us. And yet we know it's real. We know it's there. But all we see are the mere edges of the ocean.

The idea is captured in a Latin phrase found in sixteenth-century theologies: *finitum non capax infinitum,* "the finite cannot capture (or grasp or contain) the infinite." The phrase expresses that God is incomprehensible. This doesn't mean that he cannot be known, but rather that he cannot be known fully or completely. We can never exhaust him. We can never come to an end of knowing him.

The secular mind feels threatened by anything that lies beyond its reach. Science has complete knowledge as its ultimate goal. The very concept, then, that something cannot be reduced to a scientific equation contradicts the defining premise of modern rationalism.

Since God is infinite, we'll need all of eternity to come to know him—which means, essentially, that *we will never stop having questions.* When we try to understand in earthly terms how this could be, our minds lock up. We like to come to a full knowledge of things; we don't like to have things unresolved. Is this the ultimate tease—that a never-ending question has been laid before us? No, because we've been given a never-ending Answer. Jesus said, "'I am the way and the truth and the life'" (John 14:6). Paul said that "all the treasures of wisdom and knowledge" are hidden in Christ (Colossians 2:3).

God is like an infinite set in mathematics. You can count to a trillion, and then add one and keep on going. The knowledge of God is likewise inexhaustible. We can learn one trillion things about God and then add another, and another, through the infinite set of who God is. We've been called to know this God who inhabits eternity (Isaiah 57:15), even though we can only approach "the mere edges of His ways."

The Secular Fairy Tale

The Grand Canyon was still there when I came back after many years, and it will still be there long after I'm gone. But what about faith? Will it remain? And will my children's faith remain? Jesus posed the question, "'When the Son of Man comes, will he find faith on the earth?'" (Luke 18:8). The answer seems to be that faith does indeed have an end. Even so, there are two very different ways of looking at the end of faith, two very different visions of the future—the secular and the biblical.

When atheists speak of the end of faith, they're imagining one kind of ending to the story. They conjure the old secular myth of a bright future in a world without God. John Lennon wrote the anthem for that view, describing how humanists "imagine" a future in which "there's no heaven" and "no hell below us," where people are only "living for today."

> *Christians are longing for the end of faith.*

That's one kind of ending. Faith will be swept away in a tidal wave of progress, hope, and equality. The French atheist Voltaire began dreaming this nonsense over 200 years ago. And there are still those who tuck themselves into bed at night believing this is the best we can ever hope for. They're imagining a world in which we've evolved past the stage of superstition and religion—which, for them, is just another way of describing faith.

But faith, as we've already seen, is not the same as religion. And it's not the same as belief in Santa Claus. Faith is substantial. It's weighty. And it's a real part of who we are. The secularists would seem to have momentum on their side. But here's what they don't understand. *Christians are longing for the end of faith*—because for us, the end means something very different, something glorious and triumphant.

The Beautiful Vision

Late in his life, an old fisherman we know as Simon Peter sent a letter to the scattered churches of Asia Minor. Peter knew they were discouraged; he knew they were struggling with doubts. He was an expert of sorts on these very human emotions, and he remembered the tenderness with which Jesus had once instructed him. At the very threshold of his failure, Jesus told Peter, "'I have prayed for you, Simon, that your faith may not fail. And when you have turned back, strengthen your brothers'" (Luke 22:32).

And that's what Peter was doing when he picked up his quill to write—he was strengthening their faith in the midst of adversity. Peter was writing to Christians who were suffering persecution, and so he began his letter with a hymn of praise.

Praise be to the God and Father of our Lord Jesus Christ! In his great mercy he has given us new birth into a living hope through the resurrection of Jesus Christ from the dead, and into an inheritance that can never perish, spoil or fade—kept in heaven for you, who through faith are shielded by God's power until the coming of the salvation that is ready to be revealed in the last time (1 Peter 1:3-5).

I like Peter's instincts here—how he opens his letter with a heart of gratitude and joy. He doesn't start with himself or his own shrinking prospects in the world. He knows his life is narrowing down toward martyrdom, but all he sees is the "living hope" before him. Like all great heroes of faith, he is certain of where he came from and where he's going. He could look down at rough, calloused hands and remember everything he left behind—especially that long night of fishing on the Sea of Galilee when he caught nothing by his own effort. He also knew what lay before him. He knew that Jesus was alive, and that because he lives, we have "an inheritance that can never perish."

Our faith is being tested for a reason... we want to know, we need to know, that our faith is genuine.

That's what lies behind us and before us. But what about right now? What about the hard task of living in a world that's at odds with its Creator? Peter addresses this as well.

In this you greatly rejoice, though now for a little while you may have had to suffer grief in all kinds of trials. These have come so that your faith—of greater worth than gold, which perishes even though refined by fire—may be proved genuine and may result in praise, glory and honor when Jesus Christ is revealed (1:6-7).

Our faith is being tested for a reason, Peter says. The fires of suffering burn away every impurity until nothing but pure gold remains. The afflictions of life, then, serve a beautiful purpose in refining us. We cannot see God apart from faith (Hebrews 11:6), and so we want to know, we *need* to know, that our faith is genuine. We need to know that it will last right to the end.

Peter concludes his hymn by reminding us that faith draws us out beyond ourselves, far beyond what our senses can perceive.

> Though you have not seen him, you love him; and even though you do not see him now, you believe in him and are filled with an inexpressible and glorious joy, for you are receiving the goal of your faith, the salvation of your souls (vv. 8-9).

Unlike Peter, these early Christians living in Galatia and Cappadocia and Bithynia had never seen Christ with their earthly eyes. We don't see Christ now either, but we will see him someday. John tells us that "when he appears, we shall be like him, for we shall see him as he is" (1 John 3:2).

This is the goal of our faith, the completion of our salvation. This is the "end" of our faith (as the New King James Version translates it). Heaven is the end of the line. When we stand before the Lord, faith will have served its purpose—and run its course.

Horatio Spafford prayed for that kind of ending. He had lost his fortune in the Chicago Fire of 1871, and then he lost all four of his daughters in a sea disaster. Soon after, as he sailed near the spot where his daughters had died, he looked ahead to the end of faith. Spafford wrote the words of the familiar hymn "It Is Well with My Soul," including the impatient, final stanza:

> And Lord, haste the day when my faith shall be sight,
> The clouds be rolled back as a scroll;
> The trump shall resound, and the Lord shall descend,
> Even so, it is well with my soul.

A great truth lies behind these desperately hopeful words. Yes, faith really does have an expiration date, and that's the beautiful vision when we will see Christ.

As far back as the early church, we see Christians wrestling with the concept of seeing God. "I am at a loss," Augustine wrote in the fifth century, "to understand the nature" of such a vision, having only the physical experience of seeing.

The problem can be stated quite simply. Over and over, the Bible speaks of mere mortals—you and me—actually *seeing* God. What can this mean? Scripture also says that "no man has seen God at any time" (John 1:18). So how can this be?

Jesus gave us the answer. "'Anyone who has seen me,'" he said, "'has seen the Father'" (John 14:8). We are waiting for the culmination of our faith—"the glorious appearing of our great God and Savior, Jesus Christ" (Titus 2:13).

This culminating experience with Christ is called the *beatific vision*. The medieval philosopher Thomas Aquinas argued that the ultimate end of human life is a transcendent vision of God's glory. It will transcend both faith and reason, and it will render all our scholarly debates about faith and reason obsolete. Thomas believed there is something incomplete about faith because the believer always wants to understand the object of his belief. The beatific vision is therefore the "end of faith" in a literal sense; it's the goal or completion of all that faith is reaching for.

Faith's Final Demand

Faith always comes to an end—somewhere, at some time, for each one of us. How will it end in your life? Faith will end either in an abandoned outpost that lies behind you, where the doors swing on rusty hinges and tumbleweeds blow in the wind. Or faith will end in a vibrant "city with foundations" that lies before you, "whose architect and builder is God" (Hebrews 11:10).

All along God is teaching us gently, patiently, to walk by faith and not by sight.

Jesus always forces this decision upon his followers. He wants us to understand clearly what direction we're going; he wants us to know both the short-term costs and the long-term rewards of our itinerary. He turned to his disciples and asked: "'Will you also go away?'" (John 6:67). Peter answered with boldness, despite all the doubts he struggled with in his life: "'Lord, to whom shall we go? You have the words of eternal life'" (v. 68).

So we walk as far as we can with our heads up and our eyes wide open. That's who we are. That's who God made us to be. We like to see where we're going. And all along God is teaching us gently, patiently, to walk by faith and not by sight.

Someday, the greatest lesson of faith will come to each of us. Our Creator will tell us, like a tour guide at the Grand Canyon, to lower our heads. Then he'll tell us to trust him one more time—in faith's final demand—and to walk straight ahead for just a few more steps.

"Lift your eyes when I tell you to," he will say.
We'll look up—and we'll come to the end of our faith.
And it will be the beginning of an eternal answer.

Summing-Up: Faith will come to an end. Secularists believe that faith will end as reason overcomes superstition and religious belief. But God is much bigger, much deeper than human reason can ever fathom. We'll never understand everything; that's why we need faith. But faith will someday come to an end when we see Christ face-to-face.

For Further Reflection

1. If you were visiting the Grand Canyon, would you spend more time at the rim of the canyon or in the gift shop?
2. God is infinite, so we'll never come to an end of knowing him. Do you find this idea exciting or discouraging? Why?
3. As you look at the world, how does it seem that faith will end? How do you explain the loss of faith among so many?
4. Why will there be no role for faith in heaven?

Endnotes

Chapter 2: The River of Doubt

Teddy Roosevelt's memoir, *Through the Brazilian Wilderness*, was first published in 1914 and is available online. The quotations come from chapters 7 and 8.

Martyn Lloyd-Jones is quoted from chapter 1 of *Faith on Trial: Studies in Psalm 73* (first published by InterVarsity Press, 1965).

Chapter 3: In Herod's Prison

J. C. Ryle (1816–1900) is quoted on John the Baptist from *Expository Thoughts on the Gospels*, vol. 10, 218-19.

The *Jamieson-Fausset-Brown Commentary* is quoted from vol. 10, 250.

Martin Luther's letter to Melanchthon in 1527 is quoted widely, as in Jane Rubietta, *Resting Place: A Personal Guide to Spiritual Retreats* (2006), 83.

A.B. Simpson (1844–1919) is quoted from his *Christ in the Bible Commentary*. C.H. Macintosh (1820–1896) is quoted from his *Notes on Exodus*.

Aleksandr Solzhenitsyn (on apple trees) is quoted from *The Solzhenitsyn Reader: New and Essential Writings, 1947–2005* (2006), 612. The poem "Prayer" is found on pages 624-25.

Chapter 4: The Boy with the Cigarette

Friedrich Nietzsche is quoted from *Daybreak: Thoughts on the Prejudices of Morality*, edited by Maudemarie Clark and Brian Leiter (1997), 89.

Kafka is quoted from *Parables and Paradoxes* (1961), 93.

Chapter 5: Asaph's Story

Spurgeon is quoted from *The Treasury of David*, vol. 2.

Chapter 6: Windows in Heaven

Michael Polanyi is quoted (on Stradivarius violins) from his *Personal Knowledge* (1958), 55.

Chapter 9: First Things First
The Albert Einstein quote is widely attributed but seldom sourced.

Anselm's prologue is quoted from Eugene R. Fairweather, *A Scholastic Miscellany: Anselm to Ockham* (1956), 73.

Chapter 10: The Mainspring of Life
Charles Spurgeon is quoted (on the mainspring) from his devotional of readings, *Daily Help*. Spurgeon's testimony is quoted from his *Autobiography* (1898), 105. Available online.

Peter Kreeft is quoted from chapter 44, "Justification by Faith," of *Fundamentals of the Faith* (1988).

Chapter 11: How Faith Is Built
Tertullian is quoted in *The Catholic Encyclopedia* (1912), which is accessible online.

Chapter 13: A Cloud of Witnesses
Perpetua's account is widely available online and can be found in William Stearns Davis, *Readings in Ancient History*, vol. 2 (1913).

Chapter 14: The End of the Line
Augustine discusses the "beatific vision" in *City of God*, chapter 22, section 29.

About the Author

Michael Babcock lives in Lynchburg, Virginia, with his wife and two children. He is professor of humanities at Liberty University. He earned his PhD from the University of Minnesota and a Master of Fine Arts degree from the University of North Carolina at Greensboro.

Dr. Babcock is the author of *The Night Attila Died: Solving the Murder of Attila the Hun* (2005) and *UnChristian America: Living with Faith in a Nation That Was Never Under God* (2008). He is active in the teaching and missionary ministries of his local church.

You may contact Michael Babcock at authorbabcock@gmail.com.

To learn more about other Harvest House books
or to read sample chapters, log on to our website:

www.harvesthousepublishers.com

HARVEST HOUSE PUBLISHERS

EUGENE, OREGON

CPSIA information can be obtained at www.ICGtesting.com
Printed in the USA
LVOW07s1335080116

469835LV00022B/610/P